BATH
CURIOSITIES

Michael Raffael

BIRLINN

First published in 2006 by
Birlinn Ltd
West Newington House
10 Newington Road
Edinburgh EH9 1QS

www.birlinn.co.uk

ISBN10: 1 84158 503 3
ISBN: 978 1 84158 503 1

British Library Cataloguing-in-Publication Data
A catalogue record for this book is available from the British Library

Edited by Alison Moss
Design by Andrew Sutterby

Printed and bound by Compass Press, China

CONTENTS

ACKNOWLEDGEMENTS

Stuart Burrough of Bath Museum at Work for help, advice and the use of archive material; Bath Preservation Trust – especially Amy of Beckford's Tower and Museum – for permission to reproduce photographic material; David Bromwich of Somerset Studies Library for his help and permission to reproduce engravings from *The New Bath Guide*; Colin Johnston, Record Office Bath, for his patience and persistence; the Bath Postal Museum for a picture of the mail coach; the Landguard Fort Trust for a picture of Sir Philip Thicknesse; the Twickenham Museum for a sketch of Alexander Pope in Bath; Alan Gresley for the right to reproduce a Baedeker map; George Bayntun's bookbinders, for access to its photographic collection; Somersetshire Coal Canal Society for access to an excellent website, http://rtjhomepages.users.btopenworld.com/SCC2.html; the Bath Blitz Memorial Project; *The Bath Chronicle* for an archive photograph of the blitz; David Francis Taylor for permission to reproduce a Sheridan caricature by Gillray; Bruce Seymour, author of *Lola Montez: A Life* (Yale) for advice on her early years; Angus Council Cultural Services for a portrait of Lola Montez in the collection of the Montrose Museum; the Royal Mineral Water Hospital for permission to photograph its portrait of William Oliver; Devonshire Fine Art, www.antique-fine-art.com, for permission to reproduce a Rowlandson cartoon; Hallie Rubenhold whose book, *The Covent Garden Ladies* (Tempus Publishing) unearthed Samuel Derrick's work as a ghost writer; Fiona Humphrey at Bath Tourism.

Michael Raffael
2006

1

TAKING THE WATERS

Speculators, traders, pastors, gamblers, beggars, Chancellors, landowners, entertainers, travellers, they and every other collective grouping of Georgian society thronged to Bath in the eighteenth century. It was Monte Carlo and Las Vegas rolled into one, a centre of indolence and leisure.

Look at its crescents, its squares, its Circus, its Assembly Rooms, its Pump Room, its parades: close the eyes and picture the elegant Macaronis (the dandies of their day) strutting their stuff beside ladies in silks and brocades, sedan chairs bustling down the paved streets crying 'Chair!', and coaches rumbling into the city to the accompaniment of the Abbey's welcoming bells.

Seductive as the image is, mythical almost, it doesn't do justice to the place or the people who lived there or the incomers who stayed maybe for a season, maybe for a month, maybe for a few days. Like Rome, Georgian Bath wasn't built in a day. It evolved.

At the turn of the century when Queen Anne visited it, twice, it was no more than a small, walled country town clustered around the Abbey church. There were hot springs to bathe in – the 'King's' Bath

Medical consultation from Thomas Rowlandson's *The Comforts of Bath.*

Water from the Pump.

for men and the 'Queen's' for ladies, and there was a 'Lazars' Bath', dating from Tudor times where lepers might attempt to wash away their wasting disease. But there were no Assembly Rooms, no Theatre Royal, no Circus, no Queen's Square, no Pulteney Bridge, no Guildhall, no Royal Crescent.

Richard 'Beau' Nash, the most illustrious Master of Ceremonies, whose statue stands in a hallowed alcove in the Pump Room, would never have seen the room as it is now, because it didn't exist in his life-time. He would recognise little of the world heritage city that attracts more visitors per resident today than any other cultural centre in the world, bar Venice.

When the impecunious ex-guards officer, addicted to gambling, arrived in 1704, he had found a job as deputy Master of Ceremonies to Captain Webster, a stolid incumbent who plodded about the town hall where dances were held in boots.

Webster's death in a duel, fought over a game of cards, made way for Nash, a gentleman accustomed to London high society. The code of conduct he laid down shaped cultural mores into the Regency period over a century later.

He prevented men from wearing swords, established a dress code, stopped public swearing, set precedence at balls based on rank. Professional musicians were hired to entertain the public. Lodging houses rented out to incomers were checked for comfort and cleanliness, the rates they charged, fixed. Nash also fixed the 'subscriptions' visitors paid to enjoy the amenities.

On his tour round Britain in 1730 Daniel Defoe, author of *Robinson Crusoe*, noted of Nash: 'He is as one may say Director-General of the pleasures, wherever he comes is much caressed and everyone seems to submit with delight, so much is he esteemed by the regulations he imposes with regard to decorum and the economy of the place.'

'Water is Best', a quotation from Pindar, fifth-century BC poet, which can be found in the Pump Room.

By then the Bath Season, lasting from November until April was well established as the central part of the social calendar.

By then, too, the gathering of country squires, nobility, gentry, rich tradesmen and their relatives had become known collectively as the Company, its members mixing in public on equal terms regardless of class differences that would have kept them apart elsewhere.

Ostensibly people came to enjoy the healing properties of the hot springs that bubble up to the surface at the rate of a million litres a day. Physicians recommended them as a treatment or remedy for almost any disorder they chose to diagnose, from infertility to inflammation of the bowels. What the Company wanted as much as any cure for rheumatism was entertainment: from breakfast parties in the Spring Gardens beside the Avon to balls that ended at 11 p.m., they filled their days with a whirl of social engagements that flitted carelessly from the sacred to the profane.

The spa town decked out with Palladian houses grew piecemeal as speculators built to accommodate a population that doubled every twenty years, splitting the corsets of its medieval bounds and sprawling up the sides of the surrounding hills. For much of the century whole blocks of new streets, battened with scaffolding would have been part of a dusty urban development.

The famous landmarks of the guidebooks replaced older structures. The Assembly Rooms, made up of the Ballroom, Octagon, Tea Room and Card Room, opened a decade after Nash's death in competition

Caricatures from Christopher Anstey's *The New Bath Guide*.

with the Harrison Rooms that he had built in 1708 at the other end of the city. The Theatre Royal (1805) replaced an earlier theatre royal that's currently a Masonic temple.

The proto-tourists who made up the Company weren't weighed down by the awe that age and history inspire. Warts, gout and all, they took Bath as they found it, loving it, loathing it. Those with the talent described what they saw, either through images or words. Whether they were affectionate, gently mocking or cruel, they were never indifferent or unmoved by what was happening around them.

After Nash died in 1761 Christopher Anstey became the city's de facto poet laureate. Middle-aged, his health apparently broken and grieving for the loss of a beloved sister, he had quit his Cambridgeshire estates to move into one of the new houses in the Royal Crescent. As a distraction he composed a light-hearted account of what he found, written in a style that must have tripped off his pen. Published as *The New Bath Guide*, it caught the imagination of enthusiasts and cynics alike because his irony without malice gave him licence to attack targets everyone recognised. He sent up the women while they bathed:

> And then they take to the water like so many spaniels
> And tho' all the while it grew hotter and hotter
> They swam just as if they were hunting an otter.

He ridiculed everyone's favourite pastime, gaming:

> And gaming no doubt is of infinite use
> That same circulation of cash to produce
> What true public spirited people are here
> Who for that very purpose come ev'ry year

He poked fun at cooks, doctors, milliners, fops and, above all, the cost of having a good time:

> Paid bells and musicians
> Drugs, nurse and physicians
> Balls, raffles, subscriptions and chairs
> Wigs, gowns skins and trimming

BATH CURIOSITIES

Good books for the women
Plays, concerts, tea, negus and prayers.

Nobody was offended, because what he said was what everyone gossiped. A generation earlier, when John Wood, the Elder, the architect responsible for the shape and appearance of Bath, had barely begun his work, when the Mineral Water Hospital that took the poor and infirm off the streets was being founded, a forgotten poem 'Diseases of Bath', about the so-called health-giving nature of the spa, was anything but gentle about the risks of trusting a medical practitioner or buying a potion from an apothecary:

His Shop a nauseous, litter'd Magazine
Of all that is unwholsome and unclean.
From the low Roof on hempen Lines are hung
Dried Insects, Bladders, and stale Simples strung.
Here Cobwebs dangle from a Crocodile;

With unwash'd Hands each Med'cine he deals out
Pills for within, or Ointments for without:
Patients alike and Preparations blends;
Careless to whom, or what: – so he but sends.

The anonymous author condemns, even handedly, dirty streets, a weak mayor, a backbiting Corporation and people 'the scum of the nation'.

Horace Walpole was a Georgian equivalent to Oscar Wilde, a witty, cultivated aesthete. However, unlike Wilde, he was rich, noble, the son of England's first prime minister and under no obligation to earn a living. Nor was he at risk of being censured for his homosexuality. He was more amused by *The New Bath Guide* than by the city and its pleasures. A snob, he drew no pleasure from the milling crowds who gathered at the Pump or who bathed at the King's Bath beside it. Credited with starting the Gothic revival, he was unimpressed by the neoclassical buildings around him, like 'little hospitals', he thought. What impressed him more was the A-list with whom he could rub shoulders – the Lord Chancellor, the Duke of Bedford, Lord and Lady Powis. 'There are', he sniffed, 'forty thousand others that I neither know nor intend to know'. And in October 1766, that was just the Company, those who had come to take the waters.

To chase away his carefully cultivated ennui, he went to see the Methodist John Wesley, preaching and conducting a chorale: 'They have boys and girls with charming voices, that sing hymns... so long, that one would think they were already in eternity, and knew how much time they had before them'. Wesley himself was 'wond'rous clean' and as much an actor as Garrick, Britain's most revered thespian.

What Walpole thought about Bath comes unadulterated from his private correspondence, and he dismissed the spa as provincial. 'These watering places, that mimic a capital, and add vulgarisms and familiarities of their own, seem to me like Abigails [ladies' maids] in cast gowns, and I am not young enough to take up with either'.

Tobias Smollett, on the other hand, was a professional novelist and travel writer who distilled his personal experiences into fiction. In *Humphry Clinker*, written as a series of letters, he painted the city through the eyes of four members of a family and their servant. The latter traps a charwoman sneaking out at dawn with stolen beer, turkey, tongue and 'part of a buttock of beef'. Mathew Bramble, an elderly Gloucestershire squire, faints at a ball in the Assembly Rooms because of the stench of sweaty humanity, rails against the noise, against the triviality, but warms when he meets some old friends in a coffee house – a wooden-legged admiral, a fox-hunting friend with inflamed bowels and a colonel who had lost the use of his legs fighting in America. His sister, a frazzled spinster, is pursued by an elderly Irish fortune hunter. The ingenuous nephew and niece lap up the excitement of meeting a famous actor or Samuel Derrick, Nash's successor as Master of Ceremonies. Smollett may have invented the characters of his family, but he knew the real aging, drunken actor Quinn, as he had known Derrick when the gaudy Master of Ceremonies was a hack poet, living virtually in rags on the streets of London.

Richard Brinsley Sheridan was in his early twenties when he wrote *The Rivals*, the first of two plays that turned him into the foremost dramatist of his generation, able to buy up the Theatre Royal Drury Lane with the proceeds. A slight romantic comedy, it's remembered today for the character of Mrs Malaprop who has the singular ability to misuse words:

I would by no means wish a daughter of mine to be a progeny of learning; I don't think so much learning becomes a young woman; for instance, I would never let her meddle with Greek, or Hebrew, or algebra, or simony, or fluxions, or paradoxes, or such inflammatory branches of learning – neither would it be necessary for her to handle any of your mathematical, astronomical, diabolical instruments.

What the play's contemporary audience would have known is that the plot which leads up to a mock heroic duel was based on the playwright's own two encounters with a rival. The beautiful Miss Linley, whom he had married, had already been the subject of an earlier play based on her rejection of an elderly suitor. The real-life drama of a Bath scandal, entertainment for the chattering classes was dressed up to become a memorable theatrical event.

Thomas Gainsborough was one of several dozen portrait painters, rolling out likenesses for wealthy customers. His beauties, such as Eliza Linley or Ann Ford, or his formally arranged couples, painted against an imaginary backdrop in his studio close to the Abbey, gaze out from the walls of the world's great galleries in the twenty-first century.

Are they any truer a representation than the distorted grimaces sketched by the caricaturists who gleaned such rich pickings in the city? Like Smollett, Thomas Rowlandson was a journeyman professional who took no prisoners. In his series *The Comforts of Bath*, the air is often steamy, infected, smog-ridden. When he depicts the artist's studio, the fat sitter poses, his crutches beside him while his wife behind a screen cuckolds him with her beau. His doctors view their patient with the beaked ferocity of hungry vultures. The cartoonist's country dances at the Assembly Rooms have the frenetic energy of a rave, rather than the neat courtesies of a French minuet.

Rowlandson's friend John Nixon also painted, sketched and drew cartoons, but as an amateur. Like Christopher Anstey, his view of the city's trivial pursuits is kinder. When he draws a couple of pencil sketches at a concert, he might be snapping head and shoulder shots with a digital camera. His portly surgeon looks laid back, comfortable, benevolent almost. A nurse teaching an infant to walk in Grosvenor Gardens while the mother watches invites a smile of complicity.

Jane Austen's letters from Bath have the same kind of personal alertness, as opposed to the crafted prose that sees Bath through the characters she created in *Northanger Abbey* and *Persuasion*. She wrote to her sister Cassandra:

> I cannot, anyhow, continue to find people agreeable; I respect Mrs. Chamberlayne for doing her hair well, but cannot feel a more tender sentiment. Miss Langley is like any other short girl, with a broad nose and wide mouth, fashionable dress and exposed bosom. Adm. Stanhope is a gentleman-like man, but then his legs are too short and his tail too long.

Jane wasn't musical. One of the first things she did when her father brought her to live in the city was to sell the piano she had left in her old home. She doesn't write about dancing and concerts so much as about dresses and bonnets, because, quite simply, she preferred them. What would have fascinated her would have been the furore caused in her family and circle of acquaintances when her aunt was charged with shoplifting, tried and then acquitted – especially as she probably didn't like her relative overmuch.

Charles Dickens is alleged to have chosen the names 'Pickwick' and 'Papers' after a trip to Bath as a young reporter for the *Morning Chronicle*. It's a plausible connection since an ex-mayor of the city, an innkeeper who owned one of the larger coaching companies, bore the name. True or false, his narrative of Mr Pickwick's incident-packed stay has a cuddly immediacy. His faithful servant Sam Weller's comment that the waters have 'a very strong flavour o' warm flat irons' strikes a chord with anyone who has drunk them, whether or not they know what flat irons might taste like.

What's overlooked, because of the author's fame, is that his book was published when Victoria was being crowned, but it's set in a past, not too distant from Dickens's own, but far enough for a deep patina of nostalgia to glow from it. His personal view of Bath would have been one of a growing respectability. Apparently he fell out of love with it later in life because a long-forgotten play, written by his friend Bulwer-Lytton and performed at the Assembly Rooms by the Guild of Literature of which he was a member, received a bad review in the local paper. Was the city getting too stuffy or was he?

Bath was never, not even in its heyday, as beautiful to look at as it is now. What Jane Austen saw on her first visit failed to live up to her expectations. 'The sun was got behind everything, and the appearance of the place from the top of Kingsdown was all vapour, shadow, smoke, and confusion'. Come to think of it, apart from the smoke, it hasn't changed that much.

Cool Bath, *c.* 1800.

2

BEAU DERRICK

Beau Nash was dead. Toothless, confined to a wheelchair, pretty well broke, the man who had lorded over society for half a century, who had effectively created it through his role as Master of Ceremonies, who had seen the city break from the chrysalis of its medieval walls, left behind him a busy, prosperous, self-important leisure resort governed, like any club, by rules.

He himself had been appointed by the Corporation after his predecessor, a Captain Webster had been killed in a duel fought over a gambling quarrel. Nash had acted as his deputy and the selection had gone through on the nod because the position then was equivalent to that of an entertainments manager, responsible for arranging balls, dances and other social gatherings.

During his reign, though, he had created a kind of royal court culture, dependent on strict codes of conduct, where the hierarchy of social status was respected but where, in public at least, people of differing backgrounds could rub shoulders. As the man that made the rules, the one who enforced them, he had in every sense deserved his self-appointed title 'King of Bath'.

On his death, the Corporation followed the precedent set by Nash in choosing his deputy to replace him. Jacques Collette, who was French, preferred to anglicise himself as James Collet. He was gangling, amiable; a dancer who enjoyed tripping measures with children half his height and a quarter his age, a man with neither charisma, nor authority. His election, unendorsed by the city's rich and powerful visitors caused an outcry that led to the enrolment of Samuel Derrick.

Never heard of him? It's hardly surprising. His statue doesn't stand on a pedestal in the Pump Room. Guides don't point to the bronzed plaque on some elegant town house and say: 'That's where he died.' In his life though, especially before he achieved respectability by becoming Bath's Master of Ceremonies, he earned his footnote in history.

Born in Dublin, his family had planned a career for him as a cloth merchant. He had been apprenticed to a successful linen-draper aunt who was grooming him to take over her business. The youthful Derrick, however, imagined himself as a Hibernian poet-playwright, which is how he presented himself when he was first sent to London on a sales trip. There he schmoozed with luminaries such as Dr Samuel Johnson and the actor David Garrick before returning to Ireland star-struck.

Still a young man, with some savings in his pocket plus an understanding that he was his rich aunt's main beneficiary, he headed back to the English capital where he dropped any pretence of being a tradesman in order to pen plays and poems. For a while he toyed with acting. As a writer, he found few takers for his poems. His plays never reached performance. On stage, he showed less talent still. Having squandered his reserves and extended his credit to breaking point, he enrolled as a Grub Street hack, scribbling to order for the pamphlet- and booksellers.

During one particularly bleak period, no longer able to afford lodgings, he either sought the generosity of friends, or in extremis slept rough. His lack of personal hygiene was notorious. If he were in funds he might treat himself to a new, fashionable frock coat with fitted britches, but not a fresh shirt. His feet stank. Tobias Smollett, best-selling author of novels such as *Roderick Random* and *Humphry Clinker*, met him once at the Forrest coffee house, Charing Cross, when he was going through one of his worst patches: 'He had neither shoes nor stockings that were wearable'. According to the author he kept excusing himself, ostensibly to relieve himself, but in fact to conceal the holes.

Smollett recognised that his companion was on the verge of destitution and offered him work on his *Critical Review*. He also 'slipt a guinea into his hand to equip his legs and feet for the next day'.

During his London life, Derrick showed an unerring talent for womanising.

He carried on a five-year intrigue with the courtesan Charlotte Hayes who later ran Santa Charlotta in St James, the most celebrated high-class bordello in the capital. During another of his lean spells, he lived with an actress, Jane Lessingham, whom Svengali-like he had groomed for stardom and who eventually had to bail him out of debtor's prison.

BEAU DERRICK

When James Boswell, Dr Johnson's biographer and friend settled in London, Derrick had shown him the sights. He must have made an impression, because the Scot referred to him as 'a little blackguard pimping dog'. The chosen words aren't accidental. His experience of bagnios, bawdy houses and brothels together with their inmates earned him the ideal credentials to ghostwrite *Harris's List*, a guidebook to the whores of Covent Garden.

The beauty of this register was twofold. It provided accurate up-to-the-minute information for the punters on the respective charms or dangers of the ladies on offer, who, like restaurants in a guide fell into various categories and price brackets. At the same time, it provided a vicarious thrill for any top-shelf reader of the day.

Commercially, its success rendered the author solvent, with the added benefit that each annual edition (any guide must be kept up to date, especially one dealing with the passing of female beauty!) was guaranteed. His experience as a theatre critic had honed his razor-sharp tongue: 'She (Pol Forrester, Bow Street) has an entrance to the palace of pleasure as wide as a church door; and breath worse than a Welch bagpipe' or 'She is not pretty, neither ugly; but is as lewd as goats and monkeys... a vile bitch.'

The putative author, Harris, a head waiter-cum-pander at the Shakespeare's Head Tavern was identified with the book, but gentlemen in the wide circle of Derrick's acquaintances, many of whom would have had first-hand experience of the wares he was promoting, would have recognised his handiwork. The fact that no 'lady' would ever hear about this lewd volume, let alone ask questions about its authorship, was ironically instrumental in Derrick becoming Bath's Master of Ceremonies.

Financially more secure, he headed back to Ireland with the avowed intention of writing a history of his native country. Armed with letters of recommendation from influential landowners whose society he had cultivated, his reception there would have been warmer but for the fact that it was the early autumn, when like a flock of migrating geese, the local gentry with wives and dependents flew across the Irish Sea to winter in Bath.

He followed them and spent the Season there, on the one hand roistering with his mates from the West End taverns, coffee houses and fleshpots, on the other flirting with the ladies like the accomplished Lothario he was.

After James Collet's brief interregnum, it was decided that he would have to stand in a formal election before his position could be confirmed. He had been carrying out a figurehead role as the Corporation's appointee, but was disliked by the influential owners of the Assembly Rooms.

In the dash to nominate potential challengers to the Frenchman, Derrick's name wormed its way to the top of the list. Although Derrick never divulged who she was, saying only that she was the wife of Lord X, he charmed a lady with his poet persona, so much so that she encouraged her husband to support Derrick's candidature. That he triumphed was a reflection on his networking skills. To the Irish of both sexes he was one of them. The knowing London libertines on holiday in Bath recognised a kindred spirit, a fellow debauchee. Most significantly, the women admired the author, the poet, the elegant man about town with exemplary manners.

In his attempt to rebuff the Irishman, Collet accused him of low birth (true), of being short (true), of a 'want of knowledge in polite life' (questionable) and of body odour (probably true), all to no avail.

Beau Nash had established a code of conduct for polite society. Although no sinecure, the new Master of Ceremonies' role had ceased to require any law giving beyond dress code. A fanciful complaint about his daily routine states:

> When I go out, I must know everybody and smile at everybody and bow at everybody I meet; so that I suffer the tortures of perpetual rheumatism in my shoulder from the incessant motion of my hand to my head.

The reference is to the cream hat marking out the Master of Ceremonies, which had to be doffed with every bow.

Having been a tradesman, an indigent poet, a hack and a panderer, Derrick had transmuted himself into a person of means, of authority, of standing. He still composed verses, notably a satire condemning the actor James Quinn, who had supported Collet's cause, referring to him as 'Poor Guts', a throwback to the spiteful invective he had used to damn the ladies of Covent Garden.

In his behaviour, though, he compensated for his diminutive stature by extravagant display. 'Vanity had no small share in the composition of our master of ceremonies', claimed the writer of his obituary. He would strut the parades with his footman dressed almost as extravagantly as he was himself pacing several steps behind him. Then he would cross the street unnecessarily with his man in tow so as to draw attention to his presence.

His £800 salary, more than respectable in the eighteenth century, comparable to the income of a substantial landowner, was probably supplemented by rake-offs from gaming. His predecessor had fallen foul of the law by steering pigeons to the gaming tables and taking a cut of their losses. Derrick never made the mistake of getting caught.

Money lubricated every joint of Bath life, from subscriptions (entrance fees) to the walks or gardens where the Company met to the indoor entertainments. His job was to ensure that everything ran as smoothly as clockwork, down to the minute when he would stop the orchestra playing, perhaps mid-dance, by raising his pocket watch. He controlled the design of a cap or hat, the hour of breakfast, could produce plays, and receive a welcome at any house he chose to visit.

In *Humphry Clinker*, Smollett, who had helped to keep Derrick off the streets, describes him through the eyes of an ingenuous heroine Lydia Melford:

> As soon as we were settled in lodgings, we were visited by the Master of Ceremonies, a pretty little gentleman, so sweet, so fine, so civil and so polite that in our country he might pass for the Prince of Wales; then he talks so charmingly both in verse and prose, that you would be delighted to hear him discourse; for you must know he is a great writer and has got five tragedies ready for the stage.

This is the same man who praised Cherry Pol's 'red cheeks, red lips and red something else' in *Harris's List*.

The owner of a coach and four, he paid regular discreet calls on his old haunts, especially out of Season during the summer months when he was able to update new entries for the latest edition of his guide.

Seven years after becoming Master of Ceremonies, Derrick fell chronically ill. At the outset of his illness, his mistress, an actress called Maria Hedges, nursed him. Despite his varied sources of income he was too broke to pay his doctors' fees or cover his own funeral expenses.

An attempt to raise a subscription brought him five shillings. On his death, satirists who had held their tongues during his tenure, suggested that he might have poisoned himself by ingesting too much Spanish fly in order to bolster a flagging libido.

It was a joke he could have coined himself. In *Derrick's Jests*, a collection of anecdotes and witticisms published posthumously, he had announced that when he died he desired only a footstone to his grave inscribed 'Please don't piss here!'.

He would also have approved of the election debacle that came hard upon his demise. Held at the Assembly Rooms on 13 April 1769 it was described by the local newspaper, *The Chronicle*, as 'The Battle of the Upper Rooms'. It degenerated into a punch-up, started, according to the paper, by the ladies who tore at each other's hair, hats and clothes and which continued 'until the Mayor Read the Riot Act'.

3

OLIVER OLIVER

An early 'neutraceutical' for the treatment of gout, proposed by no less an authority than the Archbishop of Armagh begins: 'Take two spaniel puppies two days old, take out the entrails but don't wash inside the puppies'. His recipe then explains how to stuff the cavity with a mixture of brimstone, turpentine and nettles before roasting the dogs on a spit and then eating them.

This eccentric remedy would have been ridiculed by Georgian physicians as much as we, in our more enlightened age, find amusement in their methods. William Oliver, one of the founding fathers of the Water or General Hospital, later the Royal Mineral Water Hospital, was an eminent practitioner to his peers. Nowadays, he is remembered, if at all, as the inventor of a biscuit, although it's most unlikely that he ever spent time in a kitchen or bakery.

William Oliver, from a painting (detail) by William Hoare.

If his link to posterity hangs by a thread, what of another William Oliver, Viper Catcher of Bath, who devised an original cure for snakebite? Did he really exist or was he the mere mischievous concoction of a Grub Street scribbler?

William Oliver, MD, suffered from gout himself. The proverb 'Physician heal thyself' comes to mind when examining his ability to treat it efficaciously. He had the advantage of personal experience when describing the symptoms: 'It pricks, tears and rends the nervous membranes and tendons and thereby causes most tormenting pangs… and headaches, vertigo, sickness, loss of appetite, sour belching, heartburn, flatulence and wandering twitching pains'.

In prescribing 'the Waters' as a cure, he drew a distinction between proper and improper bathing; the latter very dangerous to the patient in his opinion. He ordered different kinds of bath for different gouts, warm ones to remove 'gouty matter', baths-and-pukes as purgatives that expelled noxious humours.

Although the causes weren't known (the build up of uric acid crystals between the joints), there were treatments that stood a better chance of healing the afflicted. Dr Johnson, no less, wrote a biography of the Dutch physician Hermann Boerhaave whose method was based entirely on a sound vegetarian diet: no alcohol was permitted, milk, bread and butter should be consumed for breakfast, plus cereals, vegetables and fruit, 'milk and biskit', more bread and milk before retiring and 'nothing salt or sour, not even a Seville orange'.

Oliver, who never pretended to be much of an innovator, would have found this Spartan approach unsuited to the appetites of the predominantly rich members of society who visited Bath to be distracted from their complaints by its entertainments as much as by any bitter pills. He advised patients not to mix milk with the waters from the Pump Room as had become briefly fashionable, on the grounds that dairy products would nullify their wholesome effect. He also condemned the practice of bottling water and despatching it outside the county: 'The water contains an aetherial essence which is lost when transported elsewhere; it cannot be contained in bottles as it will pass through the corks'.

A fairly harmless form of protecting self-interest, it typified the instinctive marketing skills of the city's dignitaries in the mid-eighteenth century. Applicants to Oliver's own 'charitable' hospital, had to pay a cautionary advance to cover travelling expenses home after they were cured, or burial if they weren't. Ostensibly created for charitable purposes, his hospital had the covert function of keeping vagrants off the streets and away from the fashionable baths. Both beggars and the genuinely indigent who came to the city for their health faced up to a year's hard labour if arrested without means of support.

A domineering personality, Oliver disapproved of anything that might undermine his personal position. One of his subordinates, Archibald Cleland, was prosecuted and dismissed on the grounds of sexually abusing female patients. In fact, he had devised a prototype endoscope. He may also have initiated the design for the earliest Bath chairs. Neither the medical nor the engineering advance would have endeared Cleland to Oliver, a practitioner who was, with Beau Nash (whose life story he had written) and his friend Ralph Allen (whose dinner table he often graced) at the core of Bath's ruling elite, a triumvirate that controlled the building materials, the social fabric and health.

His profile has been stamped for posterity on the Bath Oliver Biscuit. Its mythical origin makes him out to be a generous benefactor of his coachman, Atkins, to whom he allegedly passed the recipe along with a sack* of flour and £100. How Dr Oliver acquired it in the first place isn't known. Perhaps, it originated with an anonymous hospital cook. More likely, it was devised in his own household because its ingredients – leavened white flour, butter and milk – were more suited to patients with status than those in receipt of charity.

Arch conservative that he was, he would have approved the opinion of his late-colleague Dr Arbuthnot, that eating biscuits four or five times a day would cure dropsy and gout providing that one didn't overdo the strong liquor.

In his *English Dictionary*, Dr Johnson preferred the French spelling 'biscuit' to the more common Georgian form 'biskit' and defined the word as a hard, flat bread. Especially digestible when soaked in water or milk it was considered an ideal invalid food. A century later James Turnstall, MD, one of Oliver's successors, was encouraging convalescents to take 'a moderate luncheon of biscuit with one glass of good white wine'. Proving the point that a healthy diet has always been subject to fads, he claimed that the sick should avoid eating green vegetables or fish and that the best beverage for them was a weak brandy and water.

Atkins set up his business, baking Bath biscuits in Green Street and growing rich on the proceeds. He sold it on to another baker, who sold it on in turn. By late-Victorian times there were two rival companies slugging it out as to which one was making the genuine article. The Bath Oliver Biscuit Company had the better advertising patter: 'Take for the last thing at night one, two or more of his delicious biscuits… and you will have a good and refreshing sleep'. Or, 'Guaranteed to have the aroma, delicate, flavour and crispness of the original'. Or, 'With wine it makes a first rate luncheon biscuit. Soaked in milk, tea or coffee, its better than any other biscuit'.

Its rival, Fortt's, had the commercial muscle and by the early-twentieth century was the sole manufacturer. The factory in Manvers Street was destroyed during the Bath blitz, but recovered and was still baking 80,000 biscuits a day when Elizabeth II came to the throne. Since then it has been one of those brands that are passed from conglomerate to conglomerate, at one time part of the Huntley & Palmer stable (a subsidiary of food giant Nabisco) and now Jacob's (United Biscuits).

Somewhere down the line, it lost its health food tag. Instead, it turned into one of those biscuits that were offered with a cheese course in hotel dining-rooms a generation ago. It's a shame that it should be struggling for a niche in our contemporary diet, because it gives an authentic link to the food that Oliver himself enjoyed, albeit when he was combating gout.

What of the other William? At a glance, his story, what little we know of it from an article in the *Gentleman's Magazine*, September 1739, seems so far-fetched that it's tempting to view it as a spoof or just possibly a heavily disguised satirical attack on the doctor. If so, it could be ridiculing him as a proponent of smallpox inoculations. This, however, is unlikely because the periodical's pages contained frequent references to fatalities caused by snakebite, and during the same period another surgeon's advice – sucking the poison out of a wound as a valuable means of removing venom – was given credence.

The account of the experiment, described by a Dr Mortimer begins:

William Oliver, viper catcher of Bath, was in presence of many, bit by an old black viper or adder, brought by one of the company upon the wrist and joint of the thumb of the right hand so that drops of blood came out of the wounds.

In front of his engrossed audience, for the next hour and a half the willing victim related the changing symptoms as the poison circulated around his body. The immediate pang was a shooting pain to his thumb and up his arm even before the snake had let go. Soon afterwards he felt a burning sensation trickling up his arm. His eyes reddened and started watering.

In under half an hour, he experienced a prickling feeling around his heart, became dizzy and short of breath, 'whereupon he fell into violent cold sweats'. His stomach grew swollen; he vomited, had diarrhoea, suffered cramps and backache. For minutes at a time, he lost his sight.

At this stage in his performance the viper catcher announced that, normally he would have applied the remedy already, implying that he had had more than a little experience of being bitten. This time, 'being willing to satisfy the company thoroughly' and confident in the efficacy of his remedy, he intended to hang on until he felt really ill.

After about an hour and a quarter, a chafing dish filled with burning charcoal was brought to him and his afflicted arm was laid bare. His hand and arm were placed as close to the heat as he could bear and his wife rubbed salad oil over the hand 'as if she would have roasted it over the coals'. He claimed that the pain abated, but his pulse dropped and he began retching and vomiting again. This alarmed the physicians present who ordered cordials to be brought to him. Having taken these, Oliver asked whether he might be given a glass of olive oil or two to drink since it eased his discomfort. He was then put to bed where the warm salad oil rub was again administered. Because he complained about the pains in his back and abdomen, Dr Mortimer advised Oliver's wife to massage these with oil that had been heated in a ladle.

The treatment did the trick because 'as tho' by some charm' he appeared to recover. According to Dr Mortimer, 'he had not above two or three retchings to vomit or stools afterwards, but made water plentifully, which was not discoloured; then he soon fell into a profound sleep'.

The next morning he awoke a well man. That afternoon, however, after he had been drinking beer and rum, his arm swelled up again and had to be wrapped in brown paper soaked in oil.

Is this tale for real? The symptoms of Mr Oliver, viper catcher, seem real enough. Could he, like many charlatans in Bath, have extracted the snake's venom, allowed himself to be bitten and then faked the sickness? It is possible if the snake supplier was an associate. The juxtaposition of 'Oliver' and 'olive oil', which is what salad oil was, does have a whiff of old herring.

However, it's a true story. This otherwise unknown Oliver had devised the alleged cure in about 1730. Two years later, before his illustrious namesake had become a Bath luminary, he had demonstrated the remedy at Windsor to Drs Derham and Waterland and again in 1734 before members of the Royal Society. There's an obscure reference to a Viper Woman (his widow?) being paid a guinea a week in 1762, to test the remedy on a pauper, John Lovell, at Nailsea, Somerset.

Does the Oliver olive oil cure work? The editor of *Gentleman's Magazine* thought it might relieve the irritation of bed bug or mosquito bites. In the Middle East, it has commonly been used for rubbing on sores, anal fissures or haemorrhoids. Herbalists say that it prevents head lice in children. It soothes burns.

If anyone out there would like to replicate the experiment and has managed to acquire a willing viper, ensure that the bottle of oil to hand is labelled 'Virgin' or 'extra Virgin'. It's what cooks poured on their salads.

*There are many accounts of the gift: some say one, others ten or even 100 sacks of flour.

4

THE POSTMAN AND THE POET

'A noble seat which sees all Bath, and which was built probably
for all Bath to see.'

Philip Thicknesse on Ralph Allen's Prior Park

'Low born' Ralph Allen came to Bath in 1712 to be its sub-postmaster a few years before the building boom that was to transform the Georgian city took place, while it was still cramped inside its medieval walls. He made his fortune by overhauling a clumsy London-centric postal service whereby mail, regardless of where it had been posted, was sent to London and then on to its final destination. A letter written in Bristol addressed to Gloucester, less than 50 miles away to the north, would go 120 miles due east to London and 140 miles west again on a journey lasting at least a week that was charged for at a penny a mile over the full distance travelled. In 1720 Allen set up the first two cross posts, which grew to a network of cross-mail routes that linked towns and by-passed London.

Having enriched himself once, he did it all over again, buying land on Combe Down overlooking the city and opening up the quarries that would supply the stone that John Wood, the Elder, would use for Queen Square, the Circus, the Royal Mineral Water Hospital and the theatre, as well as the new housing that speculators put up on every plot of land they could acquire.

Alexander Pope, on the other hand, may have been a hunchbacked runt of a man, but he was Britain's foremost and most fashionable poet. Polished in his manners, befriended by the nobility, his writings conveyed 'what oft was thought, but ne'er so well expressed'. At the outset of his career, he had written an essay published in *The Guardian* (1713) on gardening, not the potato-dibbing-carnation-growing kind, but what we now call landscaping. He and other cultivated opinion-shapers believed that poetry, painting and 'the science of landscape' were the 'new graces', the highest forms of art through which nature could be displayed to its best effect.

On a pocket handkerchief, he had set about creating his own

Sketch of Alexander Pope on a visit to Bath.

showpiece garden – a three-acre site in the picturesque village of Twickenham, beside the Thames. What he really enjoyed, as his fame as a poet had grown, was advising the rich and powerful, either informally or in print, on the disposition of their large estates, though much of what he saw when he stayed at Sherborne Castle or at Cirencester Park, Lord Bathurst's property, must have been going on in his imagination since he was notoriously short-sighted.

His published verse epistle on the 'Use of Riches' to his friend, Lord Burlington, provided the mission statement for landscape designers and their patrons from the date when it appeared:

> Consult the Genius of the place in all;
> That tells the Waters or to rise or fall,

THE POSTMAN AND THE POET

> Or helps th' ambitious Hill the heav'n to scale
> Or scoops in circling theatres the Vale,
> Calls in the Country, catches opening glades
> Joins woods and varies shades from shades.

The words struck a chord with the postman-turned-quarry-owner Ralph Allen. He had commissioned Wood to build him a Palladian mansion among his quarries on Combe Down where he already owned over 600 acres of land. Overlooking the city it might catch the eye due to its classic magnificence, but its surroundings weren't beautiful. A tramway carried the stone downhill beside the garden to the riverside wharf. With careful landscaping, though, his property might be transformed to create a powerful image that anyone in town could literally look up to and admire. He wrote to the poet, inviting him to pay a visit, asking him for his advice.

Initially Pope demurred. Always unhealthy, something of a valetudinarian, he had spent time in Bath, accompanying Lord Burlington, but didn't like the atmosphere or the entertainments which inevitably would have drawn attention to his own 'spiderlike' appearance.

He did though keep in touch with the rich stone merchant. At Twickenham, Pope's house lay on one side of the road running through the village with his garden on the other. He had joined the two by a tunnel which he was converting into an increasingly ornamental grotto. To decorate the entrance he ordered some pitted, honeycombed rocks from Allen's quarries and arranged for his senior mason to deliver stone urns (carved to Pope's own design) to him.

Lord Burlington, Wood, Pope and Allen belonged to the nascent freemasonry movement, a utopian club, that had acted as an invisible cement, binding artists, intellectuals and many landowners, giving them shared aesthetic values and beliefs in tolerance, equality, universalism, civic duty, natural religion, morality. It was not, therefore, a question of whether the poet would accede to the postman's request for help, so much as when. In 1739, he arranged to spend three months at the newly completed Prior Park, 'to read and plant away my time, leaving the madness of the little town beneath me'.

A Bath poetess, Mrs Chalmers, had already painted an imaginary picture of how the gardens might look:

On this fair Eminence the fabric stands,
The finish'd Labour of a thousand Hands;
The Hill, the Dale, the River, Groves and Fields,
Vary the Landscape, which thy Prospect yields…
Thy Taste refin'd appears in yonder Wood,
Not Nature tortur'd, but by Art improv'd:
Where cover'd Walks with open Vista's meet,
An Area here, and there a shady Seat.
A thousand Sweets in mingled Odours flow
From blooming Flow'rs, which on the Borders grow.
In num'rous Streams the murm'ring Waters thrill,
Uniting all, obedient to thy Will.

She must have realised that when 'the mighty genius' who owned the property set about a project, he didn't hang about and could easily command 1,000 hands to do his bidding.

Stripped of poetical ornament, Pope's consultancy contained three practical gardening tips: study the natural conformation of the place; hide any defects; show some common sense. To these he might have added a fourth, as described in a Georgian encyclopaedia: display one's wealth in a genteel way. By the time that the estate had been made over, Allen had planted 55,000 trees and laid down 10 miles of coach roads through it. Within a year of his visit, the structure of the landscape had been completed to create the view of Bath much as it is today with paths and walkways cut through the woods on either side of the main house and waters managed to flow into ponds, basins, rills and a cascade.

The statuary and ornamental buildings were kept to a minimum with John Wood shelving a plan to build a neoclassical temple in the grounds. The Palladian bridge that is a feature of the bottom of the vale in front of the house wasn't a part of its original design. Allen, though, did opt for two statues. One, with an inscription on it composed by Pope, was dedicated to General Wade, a Bath MP who had helped finance Allen when he was a postmaster. The other, situated in an area near the house called the Wilderness that had been conceived by Pope (from an area in his own garden), was of Moses striking a rock from which a stream of water poured. Within the craft of masonry, the Hebrew prophet is venerated as a founding father, the

View from Prior Park.

'General Master Mason', and his inclusion was more than a nod to the symbolic meaning of the garden.

During his stay at Prior Park* Pope had met Dr William Oliver (see chapter 3), a Cornishman like Allen, who was the chief medical officer at the General (Royal Mineral Water) Hospital and his friend, an academic and mason, William Borlase who lived in Cornwall. From him he asked for and was sent a variety of ores and fossils to enhance the appearance of his Twickenham grotto.

The poet suggested to Mrs Allen that she should build a grotto of her own in the Wilderness. What she made, according to a young Catholic priest who saw the grotto in 1828 after the park had been bought by the Roman church, was 'a dazzling assemblage of shells, fossils, minerals etc as perfectly astonished us, the floor was almost as beautiful as the roof being composed of a curious kind of stone, perforated and inlaid with pine cones'. The cones themselves may have substituted coloured semi-precious stones that had been removed by souvenir hunters.

Pope wrote personally to Mrs Allen stating that he wished to see her finished garden as much as he hoped she would see his.

The house party that Pope attended at Prior Park in the autumn of

1743 should have been a celebration, with congratulations to Mr and Mrs Allen on the success of their stunning house, gardens and grotto. Two of Pope's closest friends had been invited. One, a doctor of divinity, William Warburton, a critic, an intellectual and of course a mason, had supported him in a string of literary battles. The other Martha Blount, middle-aged and marked by smallpox, had been a confidante for three decades, his correspondent in a long exchange of letters and the subject of his poems. More than a mistress (any suspicion of impropriety with the deformed poet was unthinkable), she was a companion who could travel alone without a hint of tittle-tattle being spoken against her.

She was, unfortunately, blamed for the rift between postman and poet that was never properly healed. A practising Catholic, she was said to have asked her host to lend her a carriage so she might attend mass in town. Allen refused on the grounds that he was the outgoing mayor of Bath and that it would be improper for his chariot to be spotted outside any place of worship but a Church of England one.

As a house guest Pope had a reputation for being difficult if he failed to get his own way. Dr Johnson, his biographer, accused him of being 'capriciously resentful', capable of walking out on his host for any perceived slight. Allen denied the charge of refusing his friend transport, saying instead that Mrs Allen and Martha had had a mutual misunderstanding. Whatever the exact cause, Pope left in a huff and went to Bristol, while Martha remained behind. Deprived of her friend, she wrote him a plaintive and bitchy letter:

> I hope you are well. I am not... Mr and Mrs Allen never said a word, nor so much as asked how I went... from every one of them much greater inhumanity than I could conceive anyone would show... they have not one of them named your name, nor drunk your health.

Sensitive to the affront, Pope replied that she should leave immediately, hire a coach as far a Marlborough and that his friend (and gardener), John Serle, would meet her there to escort her home. Whether she accepted his offer of help isn't clear, but although Pope met Allen again on polite terms, he never stayed at his house.

The winner on both fronts was William Warburton. The following year, when Allen died, he was the principal beneficiary in his will,

The Water Garden in Prior Park.

inheriting the rights to all his works**. In 1745, he married Ralph Allen's niece, becoming in the process heir to Prior Park, which he inherited on Allen's death.

Pope's house was bought by Sir William Stanhope, who systematically dismantled the garden, apparently hacking down the 'sacred groves' that had been so judiciously manicured, scarring the lawns with a gravel walk and planting a shrubbery border. The next owner pulled down the house because she was tired by the literary pilgrims who flocked to see the poet's home.

Prior Park was a little more fortunate. Richard Jones, latterly Allen's architect, constructed the Palladian bridge below the house that still stands. He also built the Gothic folly, Sham Castle, on the neighbouring Bathampton Down to add a point of interest to the view. After his death, Allen was buried at a nearby cemetery on Claverton Down with, appropriately, a pyramid for his monument, a masonic emblem of immortality that had been recommended to him by the poet. His house passed through several owners' hands until it was bought for the Catholic Church by Bishop Baines, who turned it into a seminary, and it later became a private school. Its interior was gutted in a fire during the mid-1800s, but it was restored and Prior Park eventually became a Roman Catholic public school for boys.

Ralph Allen's tomb.

*Pope stayed again with the Allens in November 1741.
**His property went to Martha.

5

FRITZ, LINA AND THE EXPLODING FLOOR

An ex-member of a Hanoverian military band arrived in Bath in 1766, having been hired as organist at the fashionable Octagon Chapel. Friedrich Wilhelm Herschel left fifteen years later with an international reputation as an astronomer, having discovered the planet Uranus. Between his debut as an able musician and his departure as a world-famous man of science, he designed and crafted the finest precision telescopes of his age. Helped by his brother Alex and spinster sister Karoline, known as Lina, who lived with him, he viewed comets, stars and nebulae that had never been seen before.

Herschel had come to England on the advice of his father, also a musician. The Hanoverian army was fighting a losing war against the French and Herschel's father feared that his son 'Fritz', a member of the Hanover Guards band, might not survive, so he suggested that he should go AWOL.

Working as a jobbing musician, he had played in the Earl of Darlington's orchestra in Richmond, before moving to Leeds, Durham and then Bath. For his opening concert he was obviously intent on creating an impression. The organ hadn't been finished so he performed a violin concerto, an oboe concerto and a harpsichord sonata, all of his own composition.

In his musical career he directed the Octagon choir in Handel's *Messiah*, taught the guitar and composed twenty-four symphonies as well as fourteen concerti. At the Theatre Royal, he led the orchestra; he played in the Pump Room Band and was, for a while, the city's director of music.

Once established, he brought Lina over from Germany, partly to run his house for him, partly to train her for a singing career. Later Alex joined them. Even by the standards of her time Lina was tiny – little over four feet tall – and had been advised by her father that she should never expect to find a husband: 'My father told me that as I had neither beauty nor riches, no man would be likely to make me an offer until I was old, when some one might like, on account of my worth, to marry me.' Fritz taught Lina arithmetic and accounting so she could manage the housekeeping. He also taught her the harpsichord and singing. In her autobiography Lina says that she learned to sing with a gag over her mouth to strengthen her voice, the idea being that she would obviously sing louder and more clearly when it was removed. By way of relaxation, brother and sister discussed astronomy.

The link between music and the stars is less tenuous than it might appear. As a boy Fritz has been encouraged to observe the sky by his father. Self-educated, Fritz was always curious about the theoretical background to what he was doing at a practical level. His interest in music theory led him to a heavyweight tome by Robert Smith, a Cambridge professor, *Harmonics or the Philosophy of Musical Sounds*.

'Fritz and Lina' statue in the garden of the Herschel Museum.

The same author had also published another magnum opus, *A Compleat System of Opticks*, which analysed in great detail the manufacture of telescopes. This latter work, combined with a textbook on astronomy that was his bedtime reading, provided an intellectual basis for what became a dedicated study. Fritz had little time for anything other than his musical commitments. During the Season, though, when the town emptied, he had time to look up into the night skies that fascinated him.

He ordered glass lenses from London, constructed a tube from pasteboard, fitted them together and started observing the heavens from the flat roof of his house. Though exciting, it must have been a frustrating exercise for him because his telescope was barely more than a toy in terms of its performance, yet unwieldy on account of its length.

Early in the century, Isaac Newton had designed a new kind of telescope: a concave *specula* mirror (the term refers to the copper tin alloy from which it's made) that, acting like a light-collecting bucket, gathered in light and reflected it back to a point of focus: the bigger the mirror, the greater the brightness of the image.

Having bought a job lot of mirrors, half-finished mirrors, mirror-polishing tools, mirror patterns 'and all his rubbish' from a Bath Quaker, Fritz switched to making Newtonian telescopes. Looking glasses are made by coating glass with a metal film. To make the kind of precision instrument that he needed, Fritz had to grind and hand-polish a metal-alloy disc so that it gave a perfect reflection.

Lina recalled that once her brother had been bitten by the bug, it increasingly dominated their lives:

> To my sorrow, I saw almost every room turned into a workshop; a cabinet-maker making a tube and stands of all descriptions in a handsome furnished drawing room; Alex putting up a huge turning machine in a bedroom for turning patterns, grinding glasses and turning eye pieces.

Each task required a combination of patience and ingenuity. To grind the crude metal disc into a perfect, smooth, concave shape, he had to scuff the surface one stroke at a time, by hand, on an abrasive carborundum tool. In those days no machinery had been invented for the construction of telescopic mirrors. To polish them Fritz condemned himself to walking at a steady rate around an upright post without removing his hands from the *specula* mirror surface until his work was done. On one occasion, he spent sixteen uninterrupted hours polishing a mirror during which Lina fed him mouthfuls of food.

To find the centre of curvature on the mirror once it had been polished, he set it on its edge opposite a lighted candle. Selecting a minute pinhole near the edge as a reference point, he shifted candle and mirror until he could simultaneously focus the mirror's edge and the pinhole image reflected from it, when viewed through the eyepiece.

The principle that the larger the diameter of the mirror, the better the view of the heavens, wasn't lost on the dedicated amateur. He realised that he would have to cast his own metal discs if he wanted to have more powerful telescopes, so he taught himself casting. Not content with the existing tin alloys that were being used for *specula*, he devised one to his own recipe that contained twelve parts copper to five of tin with the addition of brass, silver and zinc.

'All this while I continued my astronomical observations & nothing seemed now wanting to complete my felicity than sufficient time to enjoy my telescopes to which I was so much attached that I used frequently to run from the Harpsichord at the Theatre to look at the stars during the time of an act & return to the next Music.'

From a William Herschel memoir

Now Fritz and Lina were spending every moment of their leisure either building new telescopes or observing with them. Lina recalled how she would forget or didn't bother to change into working dress and 'many a lace ruffle was torn or bespattered by molten pitch'. But by a combination of passion, perseverance and innate dexterity they were building telescopes of an unmatched quality.

Having outgrown their house in New King's Street, the Herschels moved to Walcot Parade where they had more space for workshops and a flat roof that served as their observatory. From there they moved again into lodgings, probably because the hobby was outstripping Fritz's income, where the lack of a garden meant that he had to set up his telescope in the street. One night he was studying the moon when

The bronze plaque outside the Herschel's home in New King Street.

a passer-by introduced himself and asked whether he could take a look. Dr William Watson, the naturalist, was a member of the Royal Society and the friendship that developed between the two men led to the society's publication of Herschel's paper on the mountains of the moon.

Towards the end of 1780, soon after it appeared, Fritz and Lina planned another move back to New King's Street. It was to be a staged change of residence because a workshop was set up in the basement early in the next year, while the family's goods and chattels remained at the River Street lodging-house. Fritz had a major project on hand. He was hoping to cast his largest mirror to date.

Apart from his musical commitments, he had been selling telescopes of various sizes to help fund his passion. Built of mahogany, they were up to twenty feet long but with mirrors that were a mere twelve to eighteen inches across. His new one would be twice the diameter.

The mirror was to be cast in a mould of loam prepared from well-rotted horse manure that had to be pounded in a mortar and sifted through a fine sieve as if it were flour. Lina and Alex did most of the work. Watson showed up and would help them with the laborious process. He offered to pay the cost of the metal, but Fritzrefused saying that it had already been paid for.

In her memoirs, written for her niece, Lina said that his efforts to finish the speculum led him to skimp on his obligations as a music teacher:

> If a minute could but be spared in going from one scholar to another, or giving one the slip, he called at home to see how the men went on with the furnace, which was built in a room below, even [level] with the garden.

A day was set aside for casting, and the metal was in the furnace, but it began to leak at the moment it was ready for pouring. Fritz, Alex – the caster who had been hired – and his workmen had to flee through opposite doors, into the house and into the garden, to avoid the shards of stone from the flooring that exploded when the liquid alloy made contact with it. The repaired flagstone flooring is now part of the Herschel Museum.

Lina recounted how Fritz, undaunted, repeated the process: 'Before the second casting was attempted, everything which could ensure success had been attended to, and a very perfect metal was found in the mould, which had cracked in cooling.'

For Fritz snatching triumph from disaster had been a major personal achievement. It was nothing compared to the acclaim that

Tools used in the manufacture of telescopes displayed in the Herschel Museum.

The furnace and floor that cracked.

Herschel Museum garden.

he was about to receive. Weeks later, on 13 March 1781, while Lina was packing up the last of their possessions at the River Street lodgings, Fritz was studying stars in the constellation Gemini when he observed a disk-like object moving slowly across the star-field. Believing it to be a comet he reported it as such to the British Astronomer Royal, Nevil Maskelyne. Within days the object's orbit was calculated, which revealed that it could not be a comet. A new planet had been discovered.

News of the sighting spread quickly throughout the scientific community. Astronomers and mathematicians across Europe computed the object's approximate size and orbit and, by May 1781, concluded a 42-year-old amateur astronomer, William Herschel, from Bath had discovered a new planet as far beyond Saturn as Saturn is from the Sun.

Herschel offered to name his planet Georgium Sidus – The Georgian Planet – to flatter George III of England and Herschel's native Hanover. It was a smart tactical move that would guarantee his pension and royal patronage, but outside of England George was not a popular monarch. His name was vetoed by the astronomical community. Minerva was among the other suggestions, which was appropriate considering the Goddess of Wisdom's association with Bath. But in the end the seventh planet from the sun was named Uranus, the personification of the heavens in Greek mythology, and son and husband of Gaea (Earth).

Ironically, Herschel had detected it with a relatively small reflector telescope. The three-foot diameter speculum he had just finished proved too cumbersome. It never yielded up any new secrets of the visible universe.

As a result of his discovery 'Fritz' became 'Sir William'. He and Lina packed their bags and moved from Bath to Datchet close to Windsor Castle where he entertained His Majesty and the court with an even more massive telescope that he had raised.

He gave up a musical profession that no longer inspired him. As an astronomer he worked until his death, discovering the dimensions of the Milky Way, thousands of star clusters, Saturn's satellites and the rotation of its rings and, by accident, infrared radiation. Lina, an astronomer by then in her own right, identified six hitherto unknown comets. As close an observer of Fritz as she was of the sky, she once noted: 'My brother was not contented with knowing what former observers had seen.' When he died in 1822, aged eighty-four, he had fulfilled his ambition to discover something new.

6

GOOD VIBRATIONS

'Quack', 'charlatan', 'mountebank' are words that sit comfortably on 'Doctor' James Graham. That he left his Edinburgh medical school without completing his studies should be evidence enough. That he used scantily clad assistants and charged a titillated public to watch him perform his revolutionary treatments proves that he recognised how far presentation could add value to his bedside manner. That he turned into a religious enthusiast in middle-age hardly excuses him. That he died aged forty-nine, when throughout his career he had promised to live to 150, would seem to be the clincher. And yet, in an age when medicine was empirical, when eminent Bath physicians with degrees bled, purged and 'watered' their way to fortunes, his cures seem at worst harmless and often as the precursors of modern health care.

A young eighteenth-century drop out, he had crossed the Atlantic to Philadelphia where he had set himself up as an ears and eyes doctor. There he had encountered Benjamin Franklin's experimental work with electricity. The American had proved it to be an ever-present natural force, in the process developing the theory and terminology of positive and negative charges. After him, its study could become a science rather than a source of superstitious speculation.

Despite being pestered by the credulous sick of all complexions to use his miraculous discovery to cure them, Franklin opposed any practical applications of electrotherapy. Convinced by Franklin's scientific theory, 'Doctor' Graham differed fundamentally on his assessment as to its potential uses in medicine.

From his unfinished studies, he would have known of one Roman remedy for gout:

> For any type of gout a live black torpedo (electric ray) should, when the pain begins, be placed under the feet. The patient must stand on a moist shore washed by the sea and he should stay like this until his whole foot and leg up to the knee is numb. This takes away present pain and prevents pain from coming on if it has not already arisen.

The Greek physician Galen, still an icon in Graham's day, though he practised in the second century AD, was in agreement, adding that a live torpedo applied to the head would cure a headache. European doctors rarely prescribed shocking fish treatments for their patients despite his endorsement, but Islamic physicians used them on epileptics and a Jesuit missionary who witnessed an Ethiopian being cured recorded that the pain of the sting was so great that a rheumatic patient being electrified had to be tied down beforehand.

In the eighteenth century torpedo-less electrotherapy was practised by legitimate as well as illegitimate doctors. The Dutch had developed an electrostatic means, the Leyden jar, of giving powerful shocks to victims of kidney stones, sciatica and angina. In England, electric shocks as a means of soothing rheumatism or gout were the cutting-edge technology of their day. The Middlesex Hospital owned a machine. The electric ray, too, made its comeback in the capital. Half a crown bought gout sufferers the right to endure the excruciating thrill of being torpedoed.

When James Graham, having returned from America, set up his Bath practice in 1774–75, he brought an understanding of what was being called 'Franklinism' beyond the ken of its spa physicians who were locked into promoting the miraculous properties of the hot springs. Desperately sincere, smooth talking, a medical man with a mission, he quickly found favour with the Company, which was always looking out for fashionable fixes for their real or imagined ills.

He had an unlikely ally in John Wesley, who was often visiting Bristol or Bath and had influential, aristocratic friends in both cities. The founder of Methodism not only approved of electrical treatment, but had written a book about it where he counselled it for 'angina pectoris, bruising, cold feet, gout, gravel in the kidneys, headaches, hysterics and memory loss, pain in the toe, sciatica, pleuritic pain, stomach pain, palpitations and so on'.

Among Graham's privileged clients was the notorious Catharine Macaulay, who was busy working on volume five of her planned eight-volume *History of England*. Widowed, an outspoken republican, she had been given a house in Alfred Street by an elderly rich cleric. Graham had joined her circle of intellectual admirers. At a birthday party given in her honour, he had given her 'with great modesty and diffidence' a copy of his medical works that contained a dedication to her thanking God that he had been able to cure her delicate frame of the complicated, obstinate maladies from which she had been suffering.

His allegiance to her makes her the prime suspect as the author of what we would call an advertorial that appeared in the *Bristol Gazette*, written by 'A Lady who was… in great danger of blindness'.

> **G** en'rous by nature, matchless in thy skill,
> **R** ich in the art of medicine to heal;
> **A** ll bless thy gifts! – the deaf, the dumb, the blind,
> **H** ail thee with rapture for the cure they find!
> **A** rm'd by the Deity with pow'r divine,
> **M** ortals revere HIS attributes in thine!

Graham may have gone a step further in assisting his patroness, because the year after the party that had ended with a luxurious dessert of 'syllabubs, jellies, creams, ices, wines, cakes and a variety of dry and fresh fruits particularly grapes and pineapples' his younger brother William, a strong supporter of the American War of Independence, married her. The fact that he was a 21-year-old assistant ship's surgeon and she a 46-year-old widow may have counted for something.

Apart from making middle-aged ladies feel tingly, James had a battery of alternative medications at his disposal.

A vegetarian, he ranted against the 'putrid, disease inoculated meat by the overdrying, blowing etc of the butcher*… the exceeding unwholesomeness, deadness, putridity and loss of roots and other vegetables by their being sold washed from their native earth'. He condemned tea, coffee, tobacco and spirits with similar gusto.

On young men who masturbated, the effete Macaroni, he was harder than a Victorian curate: 'Poor, creeping, tremulous, pale, spindle-shanked wretched creatures! Who crawl upon the earth, spirting, dribling and draining off, alone.'

Instead, he preferred solvent abuse. He was his own best advertisement for the Nervous Aetherial Balsam that he prescribed and sold. Ether** taken internally or externally wasn't considered a drug in the modern sense. Sir Isaac Newton apparently enjoyed it. Graham enjoyed it to excess, dosing himself with an ounce a day, which had the effect (at first) of making him remarkably placid. It must have done something for his appearance because a contemporary admirer said that he looked like an eagle and spoke like a pope.

Had he been promoting his combination of illuminated nostrums purely for gain, it would be simple to dismiss him, but his medicine had a kind of wacky holistic consistency, based on a kind of Yin-Yang relationship between God as the active creator of the world, the positive charge, and his creation, the world, as the negative charge. Invisible electricity and ether were divine instruments of healing in the hands of a Scot who imagined himself to be as much a prophet-high-priest as a doctor who conjured up well-being.

He found his answer to the female, nurturing side of his medico-metaphysical equation in soil. If washing was depriving a carrot of its nutriments, then an earth bath would be a tonic for the human body. As with his Aetherial Balsam, Graham set a personal example:

> After making his bow, he seated himself on the stool; when two men with shovels began to place the mould in the cavity: as it approached to the pit of the stomach he kept lifting up his shirt, and at last he took it entirely off, the earth being up to his chin... He then began his lecture on the excellent qualities of the Earth Bath.

Later he would bury himself with a female partner so that their two powdered and wigged heads stuck out of the ground 'like two fine, full-grown cauliflowers'.

Having done enough eye-catching doctoring during the Bath Season to attract the notice of members of the ruling class, including the Prince of Wales, Graham set up a Temple of Health in London, another worldly fertility clinic, where he conceived that vibrating rich clients on a celestial bed, was a sure-fire way of rendering them fecund.

The temple itself was an immediate sensation. Writing his own prospectus, he described the location, on an eminence between Blackfriar's and Westminster Bridges within view of St Paul's and the Houses of Parliament as having a symbolic purpose. The interior – admission one crown for those who came to listen to lectures or look at the underdressed priestesses – was what brought the well-heeled crowds.

Inside, the rooms were laid out to represent a movement from the material to the divine. In one, an insulated, electric throne, twice the height of a man, jolted private patients out of their indispositions. This was a mere antipasto compared to the temple of Apollo: circular, with a dome supported by Corinthian columns, the electricity generated by giant cut-glass cylinders that passed the current to the dome 'by means of an astonishing fiery dragon'.

The holy of holies, available on a nightly basis for £50, later reduced to £25, was the chamber of the celestial bed, whose use guaranteed pregnancy. Ideally, Graham preferred it to be reserved for married couples. His lectures on the purpose of sex as a means of procreation insisted on the fact that the pleasure is a means to an end. In his bed, he built an instrument that heightened the pleasure for both partners in order to trigger the vital spark that, he believed, happened at the moment of conception. Twelve feet by nine, supported by glass pillars and fitted underneath with an electromagnetic machine that crackled and sent out shafts of lightning, it was festooned with great crimson tassels. Celestial blue curtains draped from the canopy and the coverings were deep purple. The hard mattress was made from stallion's hair. Blankets, silk sheets and pillows were impregnated with costly Arabian essences, while other perfumes were brought to the bedchamber by concealed glass tubes. At the critical moment, the bed tilted to guide the seminal emission along the proper channels.

When profits from the Temple of Health dwindled, Graham was pragmatic enough to sink his principles and move to less august premises in Pall Mall where he dropped his entrance money to a shilling. The pretence of an ethical purpose continued by day. In the evenings, though, it became assembly rooms where concerts, balls and masks were held. Illegal gambling was also introduced, but after a couple of raids Graham was forced to shut down, though he continued to give lucrative lectures on sex education guaranteed to stimulate his audience:

> In the first place… there is the necessary friction or excitation of the animal electrical tube or cylinder, for the accumulation, or mustering up of the balmy fire of life!—This is what electricians call the charging of the vital jar. Then follows the discharging, or passage of that balmy, luminous, active principle, from the plus male to the minus female. These are all mere, plain, demonstrable electrical processes.

Religious fanaticism had never been far from Graham's clinical or entrepreneurial schemes. Thwarted in his plans to provide babies for the upper classes, he turned to God. In Bath again in 1789, he confessed to his audiences that he regretted the extravagances of his younger days, his excessive imagination uncurbed by Christianity, but that he was passing into the 'mild serenity of an evening natural, and of an autumn intellectual sun'.

His verdict on himself was premature. Even in his earliest days in the city he had expressed sympathy for the Quakers who went into trance-like states. Never one to do things by halves, probably under the influence of ether, he would strip off his clothes, run into the street and give them to the nearest beggar. His vegetarianism degenerated into a form of anorexia. In his last published tract, he declared that he had lived for a year on nothing but water, by covering himself in turfs. He signed his letters 'Servant of the Lord OWL', the letters standing for 'Oh Wond'rous Love'. He died suddenly, whether of a stroke or malnutrition is unclear, but he will never be forgotten for his unique bedside manner. In Hollywood it would have made him a fortune.

*curing ham, tongues, Bath chaps, etc.
**Ether was used for the relief of many ailments, particularly those of nervous origin such as epileptic, convulsive or hysterical fits, but also headaches, gout, rheumatism, stomach disorders, asthma, pleuritic pains and even deafness.

7

LUNNS AND BUNNS

Order a Bath bun in the Pump Room for your 'elevenses' and you'll receive a glazed, sugary, slightly flattened English tea bread. Slip around the corner to a tearooms in Lilliput Alley, 'the oldest house in Bath' (except that it isn't quite as old as it's often claimed to be), and you can sample its rival, the Sally Lunn, softer, paler, more like an outsize bap, possibly an adjusted brioche – or another kind of tea bread. Partisans of each will claim that theirs is an authentic recipe, adjusted to suit modern taste, but reaching back in a direct line into the mists and fumes of a distant past.

The Sally Lunn walks the walk. It can supply no less than four possible sources as to its origins, one with the conviction of an urban myth, another based on hearsay, a third founded on gastronomic assertions and a fourth, well, an outlandish possibility.

Let's consider the last of these. Whitsun 1914: suffragettes set fire to St Mary's Church, Wargrave, Berkshire. A register, dated 1537, is saved from the flames. Examined it reveals the name of a hamlet that has since vanished called Sally Lunn. From this snippet a variety of scenarios may be inferred that would account for the cake's emergence at a fashionable spa two centuries later.

The popular story or urban myth is of a Huguenot refugee, Sally Louan or Luyon, fleeing France some time after the restoration of Charles II (1660) and baking brioches for a baker in the town. This tale has the inconvenience that no record of her exists. At any event Sally isn't a French name (could she have been a Solange?).

Also lacking corroboration is the mythical, eponymous maiden (beautiful, of course) hawking her wares about town in Beau Nash's day.

Quite a bit of scholarship, however, has gone into showing that the name is a deformation of 'sol et lune' (sun and moon) a breakfast cake that's golden on top, pale beneath the surface. This passed into the patisserie of Alsace as Solileme or Solimeme and wound its way back into Victorian books as such.

What is certain is that the name was familiar to Georgian society. In one of his many scribblings, Philip Thicknesse (see chapter 8) lamented:

Tea-time in the Pump Room.

I had the misfortune to lose a beloved brother in the prime of life,
who dropt down dead as he was playing on the fiddle at
Sir Robert Throgmorton's, after drinking a large quantity of
Bath Waters, and eating a hearty breakfast of spungy hot rolls, or
Sally Luns.

Still in the eighteenth century the *Bath Chronicle*, October 1796,
carried a verse receipt:

> No more I heed the muffin's zest
> The yeast cake or the bun.
> Sweet muse of pastry teach me how
> To make a Sally Lunn.

A Sally Lunn.

It's attributed, all eleven verses of it, to a musician-baker, William Dalmer, who delivered them warm to the gentry via a mobile oven carted through the streets.

The strands of the stories, some of them, do tie loosely together. Workmen restoring what was already known as Sally Lunn's house in Lilliput Alley in 1930, found a cache behind some wood panelling that had concealed two dolls, trinkets and a variant recipe.

It suggests that each baker added a personal touch. Nor, as the poem made clear was it a specific shape:

> And now let fancy revel free
> By no stern rule confin'd
> On glittering tin in varied form
> Each Sally Lunn be twined.

If anything, this gives the impression of plaited rolls, similar to the Jewish Hallah, rather than the current habit of moulding them, putting them in hoops and baking them so that a golden brown dome balloons over the edges.

Bath buns don't slip into the English language until a young Jane Austen writes a typically mischievous letter about 'disordering my stomach with Bath bunns'. The extra letter 'n' may not be an accidental slip. She could be referring to Sally Lunns. Nor is she criticising their indigestibility, simply implying that she liked pigging out on them.

Until then, cookery writers had always referred to 'Bath Cakes' that were eaten at the endless round of breakfast parties. Like brioches, they were eaten hot if possible, split open and spread liberally with melted butter. Bakers made them in different sizes that could either be cut up or eaten as individual portions.

Eliza Smith's 'A French cake to eat hot' (1753) comes closest to what I imagine the Company enjoying:

Take a dozen of eggs, a quart of cream and as much of flour as will

Twenty-first-century Bath buns.

make it into a thick batter; put to it a pound of melted butter, half a pint of sack (sherry), and one nutmeg grated; mix it well, and let it stand for four hours; then bake it in a quick oven, and when you take it out, slit it in two and pour a pound of butter on it melted with rose-water; cover it with the other half, and serve up hot.

By itself, this won't work. Add fresh yeast or a natural leaven and it might.

From high-status specialities enjoyed by the wealthy, to local curiosities, both Lunns and 'Bunns' have endured as many shifts in fortune as they have in the ways bakers prepare them.

The popularity of Bath buns soon spread throughout Britain; preferred to its rival the sticky Chelsea bun, which was rolled up similar to a swiss roll before baking, the currant bun and the penny bun. Meg Dod's *The Cook's Manual*, a classic Scottish cookery book published at the end of the 1820s gives a clue as to what they were really like. 'They are almost', she said 'the same preparation as the brioche cake so much eaten and talked of in Paris.' She proceeds to a recipe for Bath cakes – they should rise very light – and then observes that the buns are moulded by hand rather than cut out with stamps and decorated on top with sugared caraway seeds.

At the Great Exhibition of 1851 at the Crystal Palace, caterers sold

870,027 buns, along with 33,456 pounds of meat pies, 37,300 pounds of biscuits, 36,000 pounds of potted meats, 33 tons of ham and 36 tons of potatoes to accompany 14,299 pounds of coffee and more than a million bottles of soda, lemonade and ginger.

George Augustus Sala, the journalist who collaborated with Dickens mused: 'To the end of time little princesses will ask their governesses why the people need starve for want of bread; when there are such nice Bath buns in confectioners' shop windows.'

By then they had already undergone a kind of evolutionary split that created an extra rich London variety as well as the original. Rather than the smooth surfaced, neat buns that are stencilled out by mechanical means, these had a rocky unfinished surface, but there was little to complain about in the ingredients: half as much butter as flour, eggs, yolks, lemon zests and chopped citrus peel.

Not everyone was so lucky as to afford these. Nineteen children were poisoned eating Bath buns that had been adulterated with a yellow arsenic dye, rather than the approved 'chromate of lead'. The magistrate refused any redress to one of the survivors on the grounds that he hadn't been 'poison'd outright'. 'Who among us are safe?' fumed *The Times*. It accused doctors of conniving with poison-mongers, so that it could charge for treating the sick.

The downward qualitative spiral continued so that during the Edwardian era it had been reduced to 'a sweet bun of a somewhat stodgy type, and is supposed to constitute with a little milk, the average form of luncheon taken by a mild curate'. Its quality grew worse. The author Max Beerbohm gave this impression of an empty railway station between the two world wars: 'A solitary porter shuffles along the platform. Yonder, those are the lights of the refreshment room, where all night long, a barmaid is keeping her lonely vigil over the beer-handles and the Bath buns in a glass case.'

Sally Lunns, too, like Icarus, were spreading their wings. A writer to the prestigious journal *Notes and Queries* (1852) who, 'Partial to my sweet teacake... I often think of the pretty, pastrycook of Bath', inquired for details of their creator's existence. He received the William Dalmer story as an answer with the comment: 'To this day the Sally Lunn cake claims pre-eminence in all the cities of England.'

In his short story 'The Chimes', Charles Dickens describes a dismal evening as: 'the sort of night that's meant for muffins... Likewise crumpets. Also Sally Lunns.'

Gilbert and Sullivan managed to combine both the Lunn and a bun, presumably from Bath, in a chorus of their first full-length operetta, where villagers that are about, unwittingly, to drink a magic potion at an engagement party, anticipate tucking into:

> The rollicking bun, and the gay Sally Lunn!
> The rollicking, rollicking bun!

The twentieth century showed less enthusiasm, partly because craft bakers' shops were closing down, partly because it was time-consuming to produce, partly because it was costly and relied on lavish amounts of expensive ingredients. It did survive in unexpected corners of the country. When the food writer Jane Grigson toured Britain for her unique account of British food in the 1980s she found ones that were 'more fun than the so-called originals in Bath' in Carlisle.

The tearooms in Lilliput Alley have continued to flourish as a 'Refreshment House and Museum' or more recently, plain Sally Lunns. Its kitchens bake a modern all-purpose bun that reflects the food fashions of the day. A decade ago its menu offered chicken supreme, egg mayonnaise or baked beans à la bun. Things have moved on: scrambled eggs on bun for breakfast; toasted bun with lemon curd and clotted cream for tea and for dinner, sirloin steak with peppercorn sauce and a Sally Lunn trencher.

The tearooms' own bun recipe is a secret. The colour and the texture seem to place it among milk breads. That isn't necessarily a heresy. An authority on folk cookery, Florence White, argued that the dough was better made with cream than butter. For better or worse it does have a texture that's much softer than brioche, closer, dare I say it, to the kind of bun designed for wrapping burgers.

The Bath bun has undergone even more changes. James Cobb opened a bakery in 1866. This family business supplied the Pump Room until it was bought by a Bristol firm, Mount Stevens, in 1990. Cobb owned a recipe that was over 200 years old then, for caraway-seed cakes 'the size of a pippin', sweetened with sugar and treacle, which he believed to be a forerunner of the Bath bun that became his family's speciality.

By the standards of modern British baking practices, his was an expensive item. The dough was rich, initially containing butter for which pastry shortening was later substituted. It was unusual in that it had a chunk of cube sugar pressed to its underbelly. Hand crafted, it didn't always leave the ovens as the baker had intended. Sometimes it would be nicely rounded. Often it was flatter and half-collapsed. It was always recognisable by the nibbed sugar and currants scattered over the top. The currants were an anomaly, not really necessary, often carbonised.

It may not be tragic, but it is regrettable that two genuine local specialities once so popular that they became a familiar part of the British culinary heritage, should survive more on the strength of their past history than any intrinsic merit. According to a respected professional baking textbook, Bath buns are no different from any other buns except for a little chopped peel and extra sugar used to decorate them. That's not saying very much in their favour.

Maybe the root cause for the declining reputation of the city's one-time favourites lies with the London bakers. It was said, during the Great Exhibition, that the refreshments served were sloppy and unappetizing. Bath buns slipped from a delicious hand-made Bath speciality to a routine and characterless bun – could they have been an early casualty of mass catering?

8

DR VIPER

One of his many enemies thought that Captain Philip Thicknesse had 'the stupidity of an owl, the vulgarity of a blackguard, the obdurate heart of an assassin and the cowardice of a dunghill cock'. It's true he had an unique talent for quarrelling – with his family, his friends, the rich, the famous and the insignificant alike. He once emptied a bowl of spinach over a servant girl's head in a French tavern because he didn't like the taste. With all his many faults, he was a great eccentric, someone who charmed as well as offended.

Nothing he ever did was straightforward. If he went travelling abroad, he took his pet monkey with him. If he suffered illness – he was a life-long victim of gallstones – he cured himself either by riding horseback (the motion of horse riding was said to dislodge the stones) or by drugging himself with massive doses of laudanum. If he made a cottage garden for himself, he turned it into a tourist attraction. If he eloped, as he did in about 1740 with his first wife, it was in broad daylight, taking her from a squad of armed bodyguards.

This was in Southampton, where Maria Lanove, the daughter of a Huguenot refugee was living. Before ravishing her, he had gone to London to verify the state of her finances. He reckoned she was an heiress to a massive fortune of £42,000. Having carried her off and convinced her parents that they would do better to make friends, he settled in with his relations until the inevitable row broke out when they refused to pay him an allowance. In a huff, he gathered up his wife and children and made a melodramatic exit to Bath.

There, Maria and the three children fell sick during a diphtheria epidemic. Thicknesse wrote to his mother-in-law requesting she come and nurse them. She refused. His wife and two of the infants died. Thicknesse himself was taken ill, but he wrote Mrs Lanove a memorable letter: 'Madam, your daughter is dead, your grandchildren are dead, and I apprehend I am dying: but if I recover, the greatest consolation I can have, is that now, I have no more to do with you.'

Overcome with grief, his father-in-law died of a broken heart; soon after his mother-in-law threw herself out of a first-floor window and

PLATE XXII.

CAPTAIN PHILIP THICKNESSE.

To face p. 113.

Sir Philip Thicknesse in his prime.

was impaled on the railings beneath. Thicknesse recovered and inherited a share of the inheritance he had anticipated, but when he realised it wasn't going to be the full amount he spent years of legal wrangling in a vain attempt to acquire it.

His second wife, Elizabeth Touchet, whom he married in 1749 when he was thirty-four, was the daughter and heiress of the Catholic

Earl of Castlehaven. Her dowry allowed him to purchase a sinecure, the governship of Landguard Fort that protected the East Anglian port of Harwich. There they had produced six children of whom two boys and two girls survived infancy, before she too perished. During her last days she was nursed by her friend, Ann Ford, who became the third Mrs Thicknesse.

Having travelled about France, where the captain found time to drop off one of his daughters in a convent from where she never re-emerged, the captain returned to live briefly in Wales before moving back to Bath in 1768.

The Thicknesses enjoyed a wide circle of friends there, but they both had a particular association with the artist Thomas Gainsborough. In a biography of the artist Thicknesse claimed to have 'discovered' him while he was an impecunious, unrecognised talent painting Suffolk landscapes. He had also recommended him to go and set up a studio in Bath, where he would make his fortune with society portraits, going so far as to help him find suitable lodgings near the Abbey.

The artist had known Ann in Bath before her marriage, painting her at a time when her reputation as a viola da gamba and guitar play-er was at its height, as was the talk about her affair with the Earl of Jersey. The picture, showing her with legs crossed above the knee was a scandal in its own right, but Gainsborough had displayed it prominently in his painting room as a means of showing off his own technical brilliance.

The squabble between Thicknesse and the artist, after nearly thirty years' friendship, arose over a portrait that was promised and never delivered. Mrs Thicknesse had given Gainsborough, a keen amateur musician, her viola da gamba after he had played it at their home. In return, he had offered to paint the captain. He started. Half way into the project he invited his friends to the studio and showed them the unfinished painting alongside one of his son-in-law. Mrs Thicknesse was so let down she burst into tears and wrote a note telling the artist to hide the picture of her husband in an attic. Gainsborough apologised and returned the viola da gamba he had accepted as a gift. Although the quarrel was patched up, Thicknesse guessed he would never get his portrait finished. He told his wife that she should release Gainsborough from his obligation. She com-plied, writing a note to him that at the same time he should 'first take his brush and rub out the countenance of the truest and warmest friend he had ever had, and so done, to blot him forever from his memory'.

Long before settling in Bath, Thicknesse had supplemented the precarious incomes he had derived from his wives past and present with writing. He contributed to magazines. He wrote memoirs of his trip to France, a *Valetudinarian's Bath Guide* (in which he recommends 'Wine, and drinking to excess' and 'the breath of young women' as health improvement aids), and a book of ciphers.

Having bought a house in the Royal Crescent, he let and then sold it in order to purchase and transform a cottage higher up on Lansdown that he would christen St Catherine's Hermitage after a retreat near Montserrat in Spain that he had visited. In miniature it reflected his gentlemanly passion for landscaping. Thicknesse built his own den – the hermit's cell. During the work he dug up three stone coffins 'two Saxon and one Roman', one of which served as a water feature. In the garden, following the fashion for grottos, he construct-ed a memorial to Thomas Chatterton, decorated with a bust of the young poet, who had committed suicide. The arched exterior led to a mausoleum scooped out of the hillside. In it, in one of the recycled coffins, he buried his daughter Anna, who had been the only surviving child of his first marriage. Elsewhere in his cottage garden, he interred his dog with an epitaph that ended:

> Blush then ye human sons of bitches
> Who fawn on rascals for their riches
> Yet grudge the tribute of a tear
> To the poor dog which slumbers here.

Whether he was thinking about his two sons by his marriage to Elizabeth Touchet, is not known, but he certainly resented them for being 'rich rascals'.

George, the elder son and his brother Philip had both inherited fortunes from their grandfather, the Earl of Castlehaven's estate. This infuriated the captain because he had received nothing. Twice he had managed to snare heiresses and each time he had failed to cash in. He was doubly vexed because they had adopted their mother's family name, triply so because George had inherited the title Lord Audley.

Samuel Foote, the playwright and actor, had nicknamed Thicknesse

Dr Viper for the poisonous way he attacked those he considered his enemies. His rage towards his offspring justified the tag.

With Philip jnr, his quarrel was overtly about money. Philip had bought the Hermitage from his father when Thicknesse was about to go abroad. On his return, Thicknesse repossessed the house claiming that he had never been paid. This deceit had little on the revenge that he planned for the pair.

The title page of his next book read, *Memoirs and Anecdotes of Philip Thicknesse, Late Lieutenant Governor of Landguard Fort, and Unfortunately Father to George Touchet, Baron Audley*. Never one to avoid washing his dirty laundry in public if it helped pay the bills, he set out to damage his 'two wretched and undutiful sons' to the best of his ability. His justification begins with him reading a letter sent from Lord Audley to his brother Philip 'by mistake' which alluded to the imminent publication of Papa's book and commented, 'I make no doubt, you and I are to have our share of abuse; but we have this satisfaction, that neither you nor I care.'

'You asked for it, so I'll give it to you', was Thicknesse's response. Presenting himself as the injured party, he charged Philip with destroying his father's reputation by accusing him of fraud. He then turned his attention to George who 'dropped the name of Thicknesse and took that of Touchet, Baron Audley, two words, which have stood in the role of infamy, from the reign of Charles II'.

Apart from mistaking Charles II for Charles I, it was a cruel reminder that Mervyn Touchet, his late wife's ancestor, had been beheaded for buggery after a famous show trial in which he had admitted to sleeping three in a bed with his wife and assorted men servants.

This shot across the bows was followed up by a frontal attack on his elder son's dishonourable behaviour, accusing him of seducing and abandoning a Bristol clergyman's daughter. In evidence, he published a letter from her father announcing that 'his favourite' child had just passed away with grief. Intent on stitching up his son, Thicknesse claimed that Lord Audley had admitted being engaged to the girl and had showed him a pair of buckles bought for her.

Having damned one child for not marrying, he went into details about the 'lies' that his younger had alleged concerning the sale of St Catherine's Hermitage, between sentences smearing his character for marrying below him to Miss Polly Peacock:

... whose father and brother are eminent menders and makers of shoes, in the City of Bath, whose mother is an upper servant to a reputable pawnbroker and whose sisters are very industrious in the millinery way for farmers' wives and the lower class of country wenches.

Despite his addiction to opium, a habit that he claimed to have overcome at the age of seventy-two, despite spending three months in jail for libel, despite being accused of sending excrement through the post to his enemies, despite his gallstones, despite his faith in the breath of virgins, he managed to retain the love of his wife throughout his long life. In 1792, at the height of the French Revolution, deciding that his

Thicknesse on tour with his wife, daughter and pet monkey.

finances needed improving, he and Mrs Thicknesse crossed the Channel with the intention of going to Italy where they could live cheaply and where he might write another travelogue. They spent the night in Boulogne. The following morning they had just boarded a coach when he suffered either a stroke or a heart attack and died.

Being a foreign woman alone Mrs Thicknesse was arrested and sent to a convent, not to be released until nearly two years later after the execution of Robespierre. Before she returned to England she had a tombstone erected to her husband on which she boasted, 'No man was ever his enemy whose friendship was worth coveting.'

Her generous loyalty contrasted with the posthumous vindictiveness that Thicknesse had reserved for his eldest son, George. In his will he made a bequest that would have been fulfilled had he not died in France:

> I leave my right hand to be cut off after my death to my son, Lord Audley, and I desire it may be sent to him in hopes that such a sight may remind him of his duty to God, after having so long abandoned the duty he owed to his father who once loved him.

Was he really as vile as he made himself out to be? The *Gentleman's Magazine* described him as 'a man of probity and honour'. His apology for slavery has made him enemies among contemporary historians. He locked up his daughter in a convent, but was adored by his wife. As an old man, he wrote in his notebook: 'It is no great matter of difficulty to make a woman who loves a man, believe anything he says.' With so many contradictions in his character, he ranks as Bath's great eccentric of its Golden Age.

9

THE OTHER THEATRE ROYAL

The Theatre Royal next to Beau Nash's house in Sawclose is an impressive Regency building, especially if viewed side-on from Beaufort Square. It's been there so long, and so many famous artistes have trodden its boards, that it's hard to believe that it superseded another theatre, designed by the architect John Wood, the Elder, that had been the hub of the city's dramatic entertainments throughout its Golden Age.

The 'new' Theatre Royal.

The original is still standing in Orchard Street, halfway between the Abbey and the railway station. For the last 150 years it has been a Freemason temple. Before that it was briefly a Roman Catholic chapel. From the outside, it looks seedy, as though it had once been a warehouse. The bronze plaque stating 'This building erected in 1750 was formerly the THEATRE ROYAL managed by the celebrated John Palmer MP originator of the mail coach system and holder of the first Royal Patent ever granted to a provincial theatre' seems a touch incongruous. So, too, the inside, but for a different reason. Its imposing ionic columns, the seat of the Grand Master and masonic iconography create a sober atmosphere that's part courtroom, part chapel.

It's possible to imagine what the interior looked like as a theatre, something close to those in small provincial Italian towns – compact, overcrowded, sweaty.

The length of a cricket pitch, its dimensions and location reflected the city's growth during the first half of the eighteenth century. Wood had finished the Queen Square, but the familiar landmarks of the Circus, the crescents and the Assembly Rooms didn't yet exist.

The cost of building what opened as the Orchard Theatre – £1,000 – was raised by a small speculation of twenty £50 shares. In return, each investor received one shilling per night over seventy nights and a silver ticket to any part of the theatre at any performance. Heading the

Detail on the roof line of the building.

Masonic temple interior on the site of the Theatre Royal.

group of speculators was a brewer and chandler, John Palmer, father of the John Palmer whose name figures on the commemoration.

Theatre, such as it was, hadn't been a high priority in Bath. Wood had raised the previous one to make way for the hospital. The stage, though, was about to become fashionable. When it launched, the Orchard Theatre had to compete with plays that were being performed in a converted basement of Mr Simpson's Rooms, the Lower Assembly Rooms, by the Bath Company of Comedians.

At the outset, rivalry between the two production companies was intense. There was an immediate spat when Mr Brown, the manager at Simpson's, complained that the Orchard Theatre had poached his head carpenter and stage manager after making him drunk. It turned out that he had decided to switch camps for a guinea a week wage after a drinking bout at the '3 Crowns' where he had complained of bad treatment by Brown.

The competition didn't last because a year later Mr Simpson retired and, although his rooms continued as the principal meeting place in

Bath until the Upper Assembly Rooms outshone them, Mr Brown disappeared and the theatrical experiment there folded. With a monopoly, John Palmer's theatre should have done well, but it had teething problems, not least because of its design. Wood's domed roof that might appeal to Masons didn't provide good acoustics in the bear-pit atmosphere. The space was inadequate. Customers complained about the heat and the lack of air. With full houses during the Season, empty out of it the theatre was losing money.

It had also, theoretically, been operating illegally. Although it hadn't been enforced, a law passed during George II's reign had limited the presentation of plays to theatres that had received a royal warranty from Parliament. In London, Covent Garden and Drury Lane had licences. Outside of the capital no theatre enjoyed this privilege. After expanding and redeveloping his Orchard Theatre in 1767, John Palmer snr sent his son to lobby Parliament for a royal patent. Against the odds, he obtained it, returning to take control of what had overnight become the Theatre Royal.

He ran both it and a new theatre in the Bristol docks until he set up the first mail coach service (see chapter 10). His management style brought financial security. He employed a repertory company of about twenty-five actors, who had to shift between both theatres, hiring 'stars' from the London stage on an ad hoc basis. Equity wouldn't have approved of his methods. Having dismissed his troupe en masse when they struck for better wages, he rode around England on horseback to hire a fresh troupe of actors.

Sarah Siddons, the great tragedienne of the eighteenth century, was both his discovery and his loss. He took the risk of engaging her after she had failed when working at Drury Lane. After performing for three years as a leading lady in Bath and Bristol with growing adulation from the public, she asked for a raise from the £3 per week that she was earning. Palmer turned her down and she returned to Drury Lane where Richard Brinsley Sheridan, its playwright-proprietor, gave her a second chance that she seized to such good effect that she retired with £10,000.

Out of Season, during the summer months, the company toured. Travelling back to Bath across Salisbury Plain after a spell on the south coast and the Isle of Wight the company suffered a freak accident that cost more dearly than a few extra pounds on the wages bill. About a

Bronze plaque commemorating the actress Sarah Siddons, which is outside the Theatre Royal.

dozen miles from Salisbury, one of the actors on board the wagon that was transporting them complained to the driver that he had noticed the wheels smoking. He was told by the waggoner, a man with a cork leg called Foote, that this was quite normal. They continued on their way until, about three miles from the town, the wagon caught fire. The actors survived but all the stage properties and costumes went up in flames.

It's ironic that this should have been the one occasion that fire would threaten the theatre. Its successor, gutted in 1862, was less fortunate.

For all its 'esteemed fancy, elegance and construction inferior to none in Europe' the theatre and its audience was still vaguely disreputable. When its Bristol partner opened there had been an outcry by those who, looking at their fun-loving neighbour, feared it would diffuse 'a habit of idleness, indolence, and debauchery throughout this once industrious and virtuous city'.

Nor were they far off the mark. The management had to ask 'gentlemen' and Macaroni (the dandies of the period) not to try and go behind the scenes, presumably to chat up the artistes of either sex. Servants were sent ahead by their masters and mistresses to cover seats for them, turning the auditorium into a rowdy, jostling menagerie hours ahead of the performance. Coaches and chairs clogged the surrounding streets.

With a packed house, takings were about £140. Since the price of entry ranged from 1/6 to 5 shillings, one can estimate that up to 600 people could squeeze into the stalls and boxes. Visitors to Bath resented the fact that Bristolians paid a shilling less to see the same play with the same actors in their city.

Long before he switched his entrepreneurial attentions to the Royal Mail, Palmer had made a fortune. An anecdote of the day that misrepresents his parentage describes him on a visit to London:

> Palmer, whose father was a bill-sticker, and who had occasionally practised in the same humble occupation himself, strutting one evening in the green-room at Drury-Lane Theatre, in a pair of glittering buckles, a gentleman present remarked that they greatly resembled diamonds. 'Sir,' said Palmer, with warmth, 'I would have you to know, that I never wear anything but diamonds.' 'Jack, your pardon,' replied the gentleman, 'I remember the time when you wore nothing but paste!'

As the prestige of the Bath Season grew, so the plays and the players from the capital moved freely between cities. What the public wanted was sentimental dramas such as Thomas Holcroft's *The Road to Ruin* about a rich banker with a heart of gold, or Signora Ann Selina Storace singing one of the roles created for her by her brother Stephen (the foremost diva of the age, she had been trained by Rauzzini, Bath's castrato director of music; Mozart composed the role of Susanna in the *Barber of Seville* with her in mind), or a favourite comedy, such as Sheridan's *The Rivals,* set in Bath.

In her diary, Ellen Whinfield, wife of the curate at Lacock, listed the plays she took in during the winter of 1797. The titles are typical of the theatre's repertoire: *The Haunted Tower, The Shipwreck, A Cure for the Heartache, The Cave of Hecate, Valentine and Orsino, Catherine and Petruccio, My Grandmother.* After April 1798, her visits stopped abruptly, an indication of the extent to which the Season dictated the calibre of artistes that the management could attract.

By this date, Palmer was no longer controlling the daily running, having passed the reins to two actors: Keasebury and Dimond. William Wyatt Dimond soon took sole control and produced the kind of histrionic nights that Bath loved. When Britain was under threat of invasion by Napoleon's army in 1798, he produced Shakespeare's *Cymbeline,* subtitled 'The Invasion of Britain', followed by a fund-raising interlude called Voluntary Contributions that had the audience on its feet. Next came a scene where the children begged the help of Britannia and the show climaxed like the last night of the Proms with a patriotic rendering of 'Rule Britannia'.

The Theatre Royal could sustain the level of artistic performance but was unable to do anything about the criticisms levelled against both the place and its facilities. When the Orchard Theatre had been conceived, it was for a small provincial town with a population that doubled in winter, firmly centred on the Abbey. Those who took lodgings lived for the most part in the parades or the lodging-houses inside the old city walls. Since then the axis of the city had shifted to the north with the completion of the crescents. Those who lived in the affluent new streets found that, however dazzling Signora Storace's voice, they often faced a horrendous time getting home:

> On flinging out of the house, in the heaviest storm that ever fell… gave up one chair to this Lady, because she was old; another to that, because she was young; a third to one man, because he was weak, and ought to have it; and a fourth to another man, because he was strong, and would have it.

In 1804, a subscription was raised to provide a new Theatre Royal, based on a hundred £200 shares, twenty times more than its predecessor. The Prince of Wales was among the shareholders. Designed by George Dance, professor of architecture at the Royal Academy, it opened a year later with Dimond as its manager.

For the Orchard Theatre, it was the end of the road. It remained empty for four years before it was bought by the Roman Catholic Church. In order to turn it into a chapel, it removed the stage and gallery. It opened windows to the auditorium. The vaults that had served to store sets and props became a site for interments with tombs built of Bath stone. All traces of its original purpose disappeared.

The actor-playwright, Samuel Foote, who performed at the Theatre Royal and who wrote a comedy, *The Maid of Bath,* about Elizabeth Linley before she eloped with Richard Brinsley Sheridan, the author of *School for Scandal* and *The Rivals* composed the following eccentric ditty for Charles Macklin, a fellow actor who claimed he could read through a passage once and know it by heart.

The Great Panjandrum

So she went into the garden
to cut a cabbage-leaf
to make an apple-pie;
and at the same time
a great she-bear, coming down the street,
pops its head into the shop.
What! no soap?
  So he died,
and she very imprudently married the Barber:
and there were present
the Picaninnies,
  and the Joblillies,
  and the Garyulies,
and the great Panjandrum himself.
with the little round button at top;
and they all fell to playing the game of catch-
as-catch-can,
till the gunpowder ran out at the heels of their
boots.

Samuel Foote

10

TALLY HO!
THE FIRST ROYAL MAIL COACH SERVICE

Recalling the exhilaration of a journey on the roof of an early Royal Mail coach, an 1845 contributor to *Blackwood's Magazine*, looking back with nostalgia, wrote: 'We used to glorify ourselves in the rapidity of the mail coach doing its ten miles per hour with the punctuality of clockwork.' To him the forty miles per hour averaged by steam engines on the newly built railways were an obscenity: 'and [we] are not yet content', he lamented.

The mail coach era was brief, a final flourish before the Industrial Revolution with its iron horses rendered the service obsolete.

A French traveller in the middle of the eighteenth century noted that 'the road to Bath exhibits a delightful specimen of deep ruts, furrows, sharp stones and dirty water'. In other words, the route from London to the spa had a reputation for being one of the better maintained highways in the country.

The 100-mile journey could take a couple of days. One particular stagecoach earned the nickname Sick Lame and Lazy because its sluggish passengers always spent the night in a coaching inn at Newbury, roughly halfway.

Mail travelled more slowly still. Mounted post-boys who carried letters between towns were supposed to average six miles per hour, but the Post Office carts creaked along the busier routes at walking pace. They were vulnerable to attack by highwaymen, sometimes in league with the drivers. People who posted banknotes were advised to cut them in half and despatch them by successive deliveries.

Not everyone moved about in such a dilatory way. The rich who owned their own coaches went more quickly (or not) according to their whim. The diligences or machines, owned by the more substantial innkeepers would carry passengers between the two cities in under twenty-four hours while charging a premium for the privilege. Finally there were entrepreneurs like John Palmer with pragmatic reasons for going from A to B in a hurry and the means to do so.

Owner of the Orchard Theatre (see chapter 9) and its sibling the Theatre Royal, Bristol, Palmer needed to shuttle his actors from one

The Royal Mail coach averaged a steady 14 miles per hour.

to the other between performances in his lightweight private coach. Sarah Siddons, who made her reputation acting in Palmer's theatres hated the commuting: 'After the rehearsals in Bath... I had to go and act at Bristol on an evening and reaching Bath again after a drive of 12 miles, I was obliged to represent some fatiguing part.'

The journey, either way took just over an hour and became Palmer's benchmark in assessing the time necessary to deliver the mail on the Bristol–Bath–London route. The scheme that he pitched to the Chancellor of the Exchequer, William Pitt, was for a complete overhaul of the Royal Mail distribution. His plans had much in common with the privatisations that took place under Mrs Thatcher towards the end of the twentieth century. He wanted to shift post from the rambling carts onto the machines owned by the fastest coaching companies.

In his proposal, he showed that a seventeen-hour journey was actually taking about forty. Moving the mail to private transporters would cost the Post Office no more than the three pennies per mile that it was already costing them. As protection, he suggested that an armed guard, typically an ex-soldier, should travel next to the coachman. What really endeared his presentation to Pitt was the revenue-raising implications. Palmer believed that Members of Parliament and Peers of the Realm who had hitherto been able to send letters free of charge should lose their exemption. Also, he proposed an increase in postal charges on the grounds that customers would receive a swifter, more efficient, more reliable service.

The mail coach entering Bath.

The Treasury liked the idea, but there was a change of government and then the two Postmasters General composed a lengthy rebuttal of the plan, arguing that it was expensive, unworkable, unsafe. They objected to the choice of the Bath road for the test run on the grounds that it was in too good repair. However, over two years later in July 1784, under pressure from Pitt, once again in power, the Postmasters General agreed that:

> … being inclined to make an experiment for the more expeditious conveyance of mails of letters by stage-coaches, machines etc, [they] have been pleased to order that a trial shall be made upon the road between London and Bristol to commence at each place on Monday, the 2nd August next.

This was twenty-four hours after the Treasury had announced an increase in postal charges. Pitt had a vested interest in a trouble-free run.

In the days leading up to the maiden voyage, Palmer closed deals with five innkeepers who would be responsible for changing the horses en route and assuring refreshments for the four passengers that the coach would carry. On schedule, a coach left the Rummer Tavern, Bristol at 16.00, stopped at the Three Tuns, Bath and travelled overnight to its destination, the Swan with Two Necks, in the City for 08.00. The return journey began twelve hours later ending with the coach safely back in Bristol at 12.00. Each way, the trip had lasted sixteen hours.

An apocryphal story claims that 'Coach No 1' left the Lamb in Stall Street, close by the Pump Room, on Friday, 6 August, driven by John Dover (the landlord) with Palmer himself riding shotgun as far as Marlborough. If it's true then it's no more than one might expect from a man who believed in hands-on management.

By the end of the month it was clear that Palmer would receive the go-ahead to expand his network beyond the Bath road, but not without further obstruction by the Post Office. Handing over letters that had arrived at the clearing house was delayed. Postmasters around the country received unwarranted pay rises for continuing the slow cart and horse services, but willy-nilly the web of coach routes continued to spread to the south coast and then to the north.

If the delivery of letters improved dramatically, it had little effect on the general public but improved the service to merchants, lawyers, politicians and the rich who generated most of the correspondence. Regional newspapers had to rethink their deadlines; news travelled from the capital to the provinces faster. As the numbers of mail coaches multiplied many towns received daily postal deliveries.

The other major beneficiaries were the inns and the coaching companies. Horses required feeding and grooming. Passengers demanded refreshments. The cost of a single ticket from Bath cost £1.8.0 – children in the lap travelled for fourteen shillings. Luggage was charged extra. Only the turnpike toll-gates lost out, as the Royal Mail passed through free of charge.

Unlike the driver employed by the firm operating the coach, guards were Post Office employees who proved to be the effective deterrent to highway robbery that Palmer had envisaged. The mails ran for seven years before the first successful attack by a highwayman.

Apart from a cutlass and a pair of pistols, the guards' arm of choice, always carried, was the blunderbuss, a brass-barrelled gun originally designed for naval boarding parties that sprayed a lethal charge of metal balls. Perhaps through boredom or more likely in response to tipping by younger passengers, guards earned a reputation for firing their miniature canons without provocation. The problem grew so serious that Parliament had to enact a law fining guards £5 for firing a blunderbuss for any reason other than defence.

They were also the timekeepers, checking the times between stages. They blew the horns that warned inns of their imminent arrival, toll-keepers to open the gates and any other road transport to give way.

Responsible for the mail's safe keeping, they were enjoined to ride on to the next stage with it by horse if the coach broke down. It was a felony to stop a coach that had an untouchable status equivalent to the diplomatic bag. Guards often exploited this immunity to smuggle game, particularly between hostelries, illegal in England at the time, as a means of supplementing an income already dependent on tips.

Drivers worked for the innkeeper who owned the coach. With half or more of the journey spent during the hours of darkness, with only the carriage lamps whose light didn't reach beyond the lead horses, they were exceptionally skilled. They controlled the reins for each horse with a single finger, giving rise to the expression 'four in hand'.

They sat on a box seat that was neither upholstered nor sprung to prevent the unlikely event of their falling asleep at the wheel – so to speak. Palmer intended that the mails would not allow any outside passengers. Over time, first one, then up to three fares were permitted. This provided coachmen with a lucrative sideline in that many could be bribed to let someone 'take the reins'.

Palmer used his personal coach for the initial run, presumably the same vehicle that had shunted his actors back and forth. It weighed less than a ton. About eleven feet long by five feet wide, it became the basis for future Royal Mail design. The luggage was stowed under the driver's seat, with the mail packed away in the rear in a locked compartment under the guard's feet. The coach fitted to a welded steel body in the form of a letter C that was attached to the carriage chassis with leather strapping. This might not have prevented the jolting and jarring but would have mitigated its worst effects. Between each journey, coaches were cleaned, checked and axles greased.

Conditions inside were cramped, offering passengers less leg- or elbowroom than today's budget airlines. Stopping was so infrequent that ladies carried a specially designed chamber pot, usually with a fitting lid, the bordalou.

The key to meeting the schedule was organisation. Teams of horses were changed every ten miles. The ostlers and grooms, often scrabbling in dimly lit yards, were allowed five minutes. Guards kept time sheets for the main stages: Bristol, Bath, Calne, Marlborough, Thatcham, Brentford, London. Thanks to improvements to the road, the Mail had cut the journey time to fourteen hours by the turn of the century.

Palmer, like Ralph Allen before him who had developed the cross posts, had seen an opportunity to make a personal fortune by improving a public service, but his rewards were slow in coming. He had financed the enterprise out of his own pocket. A year on, he was made Surveyor and Comptroller General in the Post Office, in effect its managing director, but his salary wasn't set until the following year, together with a 2½ per cent of revenue, over £240,000, backdated twelve months.

In the meantime, he had been forced to sell other financial interests, had £4,000 debts and his bank was refusing him additional credit. Once he started to receive the payment that had been agreed, his finances improved, but he was never at ease working under the jurisdiction of the Postmasters General. Following a series of rows over the extent of his authority, they suspended him in 1792, cancelling his entitlement to a share of turnover and substituting it with a flat fee of £3,000 per year.

Forced into retirement, he spent much of his remaining energy appealing to Parliament for compensation. Almost incidentally, he was twice elected mayor of Bath and became its MP while in his sixties. It was his son, Major-General Charles Palmer, a past aide-de-camp of the Prince Regent and enjoying influence at court, who persuaded the Commons to stump up £50,000 plus the contested 2½ per cent of revenues.

He lived a shameless capitalistic life, doing deals, chasing big money. He created the ethos of speed and efficiency for the Post Office that the industrial era would echo, but without the smoke, the smog and grim social conditions that it caused. He died in 1818.

Those who sent letters by mail coach could not help but admire it. Those who endured the shaking inside the carriage probably loathed every minute of the ride. For the drivers and economy travellers on the box it was often an unforgettable experience:

> These mail coaches of Mr Palmer... first revealed to me the glory of motion: suggesting at the same time an undersense not unpleasurable of possible though indefinite danger; secondly through grand effects for the eye between lamplight and the darkness on solitary roads; thirdly through animal beauty and power so often displayed in the class of horses selected for this mail service; fourthly through the conscious presence of a central intellect that in the midst of vast distances, of storms, of darkness, of night, overruled all obstacles into one steady co-operation in a national result.

11

SOMETHING OLD, SOMETHING NEW, SOMETHING LOVED, SOMETHING NEGLECTED

> Raffling and fiddling and
> piping and singing
> There's rare dogs in Bath.
> *Refrain from the Bath Teazer*

It's one of those myths that cling to Bath like algae in the waters: Dr Radcliffe, Royal Physician to Queen Anne, had visited Bath with Her Majesty early in her reign and disapproved of the hygiene at the baths. The sick, the infected and the plain mucky were all bathing together. Commoners used the same waters as the nobility. He threatened to throw a venomous toad into the King's Bath to teach the City Fathers a lesson. Whether the amphibian story is true or not, he did have a vested interest in bringing fashionable society to the rival spa town of Tunbridge Wells, which was much closer to the capital.

When Beau Nash became the Master of Ceremonies in 1705, one of his earliest moves was to hire professional London musicians to replace the itinerants and rustics who had been performing in what was still a small provincial centre. With a flare for public relations he announced that they would fiddle the toad out of the water.

The Pump Room Band – not an orchestra originally – has gone through many changes. Today, as the Pump Room Trio (and sometime quartet), it carries on a tradition of uninterrupted public service music going back three centuries. During that time its nature has shifted to reflect the image that Bath has tried to project to itself and to the outside world.

To the progressively crowded, progressively noisy throng of Georgian invalids, socialites, their dogs and their bath chairs, who surfaced every morning between eight and ten o'clock, the assorted performers playing on wind and string instruments and a kettle drum must have been as easy listening as a Tannoy in a busy shopping mall. Even in the Grand Pump Room that reopened in 1799 it was all

Pump Room Trio, or rather Quartet!

but impossible 'to hear their tweedle dum and tweedle dee above the hubbub'.

Their role, then as now, didn't end when the crowds moved on. The musicians, to earn a living, had to teach privately, play in concerts, at the theatre, and at the balls held in the Assembly Rooms where at least they would enjoy an audience.

These weekly Dress Balls were, in modern jargon, 'a game of two halves'. During the formal dances couples, who took the floor according to precedence determined by rank, performed cotillions and minuets, with a stiffness that shocked one French observer: 'The English Nation of both sexes look as grave when they are dancing, as if they were attending the Solemnity of a Funeral.'

This all changed when the eleven musicians in the gallery shifted tempo for the country dances. In mid-Georgian times, the ladies who wore hoops inside their gowns retired to separate apartments to remove them, but by Jane Austen's day the dresses allowed free movement to indulge in romps that had been composed especially for the Company – Bath Frolick, Bath Races, Mrs Pulteney's Fancy and Bath Teazer.

Remembering the steps to the many reels must have been as mind-boggling for a new arrival as learning to knit blindfold: 'Cast off two couples, up again, four hands half round at top, back again, lead down the middle, up again and cast off one couple, right and left at the top' (a country dance called The New Pompe Room).

To earn a good living in Bath musicians needed to turn their hand to more than one instrument. William Herschel (see chapter 5), who was briefly director of music before Rauzzini, arrived as organist, was encouraged to join the Pump Room Band as an oboist, and filled in at the theatre on harpsichord.

They were also responsible to the impresario who directed the concerts. Venanzio Rauzzini, an internationally famous castrato for whom Mozart had composed a jubilate, held sway over the oratorios and operas until his death in 1810. He was able to bring personal friends to the booming town, such as Joseph Haydn or his pupil, the diva Selina Storace, who erected a monument to him in the Abbey after his death.

Gala nights bowled over some members of the audience, such as Edmund Rack who helped found the Bath Society in the city, for the encouragement of Agriculture, Planting, Manufactures, Commerce, and the Fine Arts:

> The most brilliant Assembly my eyes ever beheld. The Elegance of the room, illuminated by 480 wax Candles & the blaze of Jewels, and the inconceivable Harmony of near 40 Musicians, some of whom are the finest hands in Europe, added to the rich attire of about 800 Gentlemen and Ladies, was, altogether, a scene of which no person who never saw it can form any adequate idea &. La Motte and Fischer surpass all description. On the violin and oboe they are not equall'd by any performer in Europe. Rauzzini is a Eunuch and has a fine shrill Pipe.

Concerts weren't always as magnificent and often rich patrons or amateur enthusiasts such as Thomas Gainsborough, a keen viola da gamba player, were allowed to play alongside the professional players.

Not everyone succumbed to the musical output of this prosperous city. The character of Timothy Testy, the Victor Meldrew of the Regency, complained:

> The Concert… Sat two hours in cold, silence, and darkness, by way of securing a place… i.e. an opportunity of estimating the inferiority of Bath to London, in the harmonic department. On the precious Concert-night, you must know, I had stood, almost the whole evening; till, at length, I had the good luck to find a vacant seat, immediately under a huge chandelier!… Mem: my new black coat presently turned to grey by the tears of the candles.

By the end of the Regency period, Bath, the fun-loving pleasure resort was beginning to mothball itself. In Darwinian terms, it had fulfilled its evolutionary role and had nowhere to go. The court had already forsaken it for bathing on Brighton's beaches. The appetites of those who still came in numbers were more provincial, less extravagant. The social climate, too, was edging towards the formal, colder, disciplined behaviour that characterised the Victorian era. Music no longer oiled the daily routine. Almost in relief and exhaustion the spa sank back into its previous incarnation as a county town, while around the country new industrial cities bursting with civic pride and enthusiasm multiplied.

If it had chosen any period in which to lie quiescent, it could have chosen worse. Seen from the continent, England was 'das Lande ohne Musick' (the land without music). It was a view endorsed by an all-powerful *Times* critic, James William Davison, whose passion for Liszt, Chopin, Schubert, Mendelssohn and, above all, Beethoven blinded him to home-grown talent.

At the same time, seen through sceptical eyes, there was a suspicion that bel canto was overblown and faintly ridiculous:

> It was a beautiful duet: first the small gentleman asked a question, and then the tall lady answered it; then the small gentleman and the tall lady sang together most melodiously; then the small gentleman went through a little piece of vehemence by himself, and got very tenor indeed, in the excitement of his feelings, to which the tall lady responded in a similar manner; then the small gentleman had a shake or two, after which the tall lady had the same, and then they both merged imperceptibly into the original air: and the band wound themselves up to a pitch of fury, and the small gentleman handed the tall lady out, and the applause was rapturous.

> Charles Dickens, *Sketches by Boz*

Despite this, music as light entertainment was flourishing, privately in parlours and living rooms, publicly in music halls, on bandstands (as in Victoria Park) and also in spas. Harrogate in Yorkshire, a genteel version of Bath in its fashionable heyday, had from the mid-1870s its own Promenade Concerts played by a small professional orchestra, led by a military bandmaster Sidney Jones, and later by his celebrated son Sydney. From playing a hotchpotch of overtures, suites, rhapsodies, selections from operettas, medleys, theatre incidental music, marches, dances, novelty pieces and songs, it graduated to playing symphonies.

Bath hadn't exactly declined into a backwater. Charles Hallé turned down the chance of becoming its musical director in order to go to Manchester where he founded the Hallé orchestra. It was in the league of provincial destinations, on a par with Folkestone and Bradford; touring companies such as the D'Oyly Carte gave a performance of Gilbert and Sullivan's *Iolanthe* at the Theatre Royal in 1883. As a favour, the company allowed two of its principals to sing at a benefit concert for the Grand Pump Room's conductor W.E. Salmon. 'Some pianoforte solos in good taste' were played by the *Iolanthe* conductor, too, and much admired by Bathonians.

In Edwardian times, the council still considered it worthwhile to subsidise a sizeable sinfonietta that played the established classical repertoire. It was still doing so when its German conductor shot himself in the right temple in 1910. Max Heyman had returned to the city after treatment in Germany for a series of nervous illnesses that would today be diagnosed as acute depression. In a detailed suicide letter to the coroner he claimed that his health made it impossible 'to do my work at the Pump Room to which I have all along been devotedly attached'.

'Probably', he added, 'the jury will return a verdict of temporary insanity as they normally idiotically do.' He was right; they did.

One of the professional musicians in his ensemble, Signor Semprini, had a precociously talented son, Alberto, a pianist and cellist whom he sent to the Verdi conservatory in Milan. The young man returned to front the BBC radio programme 'Semprini Serenade' that ran for twenty-five years playing and conducting the light orchestral music that has been a hallmark of the Pump Room Trio for over fifty years. The famous catch-phrase 'Something old, something new, something loved, something neglected' with which he opened his programme, would have been as true for its musicians as it was for him.

Heyman's immediate successors persisted with the city's ambitions to make Bath into a serious musical centre, but fate seemed to be conspiring against them. Frank Tapp, who took over from Heyman, was Bath-born. Still in his twenties, a winner of the Royal College of Music's composition prize, he was able on occasion to command an orchestra of forty musicians, giving the first West Country performance of Elgar's *Enigma Variations*. Just before the outset of the Great War, he left with the reputation for being 'too much of an autocrat'.

Under Jan Hurst the orchestra shrank to a septet, fewer musicians than there had been in the reign of Beau Nash, but he left one unique legacy. On the first occasion that he played César Franck's 1st Symphony to a Pump Room audience, an elderly lady dropped dead. On the second occasion the orchestra's cellist stumbled while climbing on to the platform, and broke a leg. The third time it was performed, someone drowned in the baths. After that, he never played it again in

Bath. The Trio is rooted in the inter-war period when ladies in hats sipped Darjeeling and nibbled on a bun in what had turned into a glorified tearoom. The music, typical of its Palm Court era mixed up the 'Meet Me When The Dew Is On The Roses' and 'Only a Bluebell' melodies of the Victorian salon with arrangements of 'Old Man River' and the 'Tombeau de Couperin'. It's the kind of hors d'oeuvre that still goes down well with the crush of visitors who pay for a glass of the waters that used to be given away or eat in what's become a grandiose coffee shop.

Paradoxically, modern Bath has, through its annual Festival, reinvented a musical reputation for itself. Conceived in 1938, creaking into existence a decade later, it developed an identity when the violinist Yehudi Menuhin became its artistic director in 1959. This has changed from a serious classical event into a kind of fairground of world music where the Festival and its fringe overlaps, representative of the glamorous amusement park that the city has again become.

12

MARKET DAY

'To pay on the nail', if the plaque in the Guildhall Market is to be
believed, is a saying that derived from the stone baluster table on
which traders sealed their bargains. Well, yes and no. The story is
more than an urban myth, but the phrase was
current in medieval days. At fairs a stick was stuck in the ground with
a platform on it, that gave the appearance of a nail. After a deal was
struck, the money was placed on the board, hence the expression.

Anon

Bath's original Guildhall, a Stuart building designed by Inigo Jones,
stood a little closer to the Abbey than the Georgian counterpart
that replaced it. Set on raised pillars, its scale reflected the numbers
living inside the small, walled city, and the market, held underneath it
at ground level, matched their frugal needs.

'The Nail' in the covered market.

Entrance to the Victorian covered market.

During the transforming building boom, the city walls were dismantled, the old Guildhall was flattened. A new market location, open to the elements, sprawled from the White Lion, one of the smarter coaching inns, back almost to the River Avon. At its core was the shambles where animals were slaughtered and flayed before the carcasses passed to the butchers' stalls. Bread was sold next to them and fish near the Abbey along with fruit and vegetables.

Its shambolic nature did improve after the Corporation tried to bring a little order. Vegetable wholesalers lined the river. An area was set aside for butter and poultry. Retail greengroceries, under cover, were marketed by the Guildhall and a separate fish market was opened next to a lock-up. The abattoir was moved away from the central area. Pork butchers were given a corner of their own.

When Horace Walpole, the creator of neo-Gothic fashion, visited the city he despised its Palladian 'hospital' architecture and the 'vulgarisms and familiarities' of its manners. However, a connoisseur of fine food, he thought 'the provisions better than ever I tasted'.

This was hardly surprising. Bristol, England's chief port at that time, was on its doorstep. Luxury goods – tea, coffee, chocolate, sugar, wine and live turtles – were abundant. The Severn Estuary that widens into the Bristol Channel was less than a day's drive away by wagon. It supplied fresh flat fish, salmon and shrimps, caught in horn-shaped withy baskets or putts, that formed a barrier across the tidal water: Quinn was especially partial to John Dory.

Mutton was fattened on Lansdown Hill. Beef was plentiful. Neighbouring Wiltshire was famed for its pork, bacon and hams. There was butter to spread on warm Sally Lunns at the endless round of breakfast parties. There was also Cheddar and Bath's own soft cheese. Poultry could be elevated to a level of exoticism that would be impossible today; pastry cooks who dealt in baked savoury as well as sweet goods sold chickens 'fatted with chopped almonds and raisins and sold at two guineas a couple'.

Though nothing was in short supply for those with the means to pay for it, profiteering was commonplace. In 1765 the *Chronicle* complained of the 'illegal practices by the town butchers and poulterers', who, it seems, created a cartel whereby they bought the prime meat in the market 'leaving the refuse to be vended'. They were then able to charge what they liked, ensuring that households with the biggest budgets received the best produce.

Mrs Martha Bradley, 'late of Bath', author of the *British Housewife*, would probably have been one of their better customers. Her book, first published as a series of weekly pamphlets over a century before Mrs Beeton, was unique in treating food seasonally. It was a collection of recipes, but also a guide to availability that shows how varied the choice of raw materials was for those who could afford it.

'Cherries', she advised her readers in July, 'are in their great perfection, the large Duke, the Heart and the Carnation Cherries are in their perfection, and the black cherries begin to come in. The Kentish cherry is also now very fine and excels many of the others for various uses; and for curious desserts, the Amber Heart and White Spanish are now to be had in their prime order.'

Her monthly catalogues of ingredients for sale show that the Georgian cook was as beholden to her herbs and vegetables as to her roasts and beefsteaks. In February, she had access to 'small salleting' (mixed baby salad leaves that the French call mesclun), chervil, sorrel,

Pulteney Bridge. There was an ice-cream shop here in the eighteenth century.

cultivated mushrooms and forced asparagus, as well as to the greens and root vegetables we take for granted.

Market gardens were everywhere, nearly. Not long after it was built, a certain Sir Peter Rivers Gay was thwarted in his attempt to turn the fields in front of the Royal Crescent into a vegetable patch.

Purveyors also handled specialist goods. Mrs Bradley would have had little difficulty acquiring virgin olive oil to anoint her 'sallets' and 'salmagundis'. Batheaston had the reputation for supplying truffles, though probably the summer variety, not the more highly prized Périgord one.

On Pulteney Bridge, known as the New Bridge when it was first opened, was Benjamin Ford's New Ice Cream Shop that offered 'all kinds of different flavoured ices, made from the best sweetmeats, essence, and fruits'. These would have been for delivery to private homes, but chance customers could pay four pence for 'ice creams of all kinds in small glasses'.

The White Lion, White Hart, Lamb, Three Tuns, Bear, Christopher and York inns, more like hotels, employed cooks who prepared meals through the day and into the night. Gentlemen's private dining clubs met there. Like outside caterers, they delivered dinners to lodgings.

Master Gill, Bath's finest pastry cook, was fêted in prose and verse:

> Of all the cooks the world can boast
> However great their skill,
> To bake, or fry, to boil or roast,
> There's none like Master Gill.

> (Christopher Anstey, *The New Bath Guide*)

His shop in Wade's Passage, wasn't what we would call a restaurant, but it was a respectable establishment where ladies, if they were escorted, might go for a bowl of vermicelli soup, a jelly, tart or a cream.

Some of the lodgings where wintering visitors stayed provided cooks for them. According to the architect John Wood, the Elder, no city in the world could be 'furnished with better and cleaner cook maids'. He claimed that it was a kind of nursery for breeding them, that families who hired these cook maids for the Season often employed them as part of their retinue when they departed.

Typical is the fulsome praise of a Shropshire lady staying at a lodging-house:

> We were supplied with excellent eatables at breakfast, even an elegant dinner, never less than two good dishes and a pudding or tart.

Mrs Bradley's recipe for a stuffed Polish Chicken from the *British Housewife* shows the technique:

> Cut a quantity of fine fat bacon for larding, and cut also four anchovies taking out the bones. Choose a fine chicken, and when picked and drawn, lard it with the bacon and anchovies, a piece of one and a piece

of the other; and when this is done, strew over the whole a quantity of sweet herbs and spices shred and mixed together. Cut the liver of the chicken small, and mix with it some parsley, three truffles, a slice of bacon minced small, the yolks of two eggs, and a blade of mace pounded; mix well together then strew in a very little pepper and salt; when all this is perfectly well mixed, fill the body of the chicken with it, and lay it down to roast at a moderate distance from a very good fire. When the chicken is half done heat a clean fire shovel till it is just red hot, then let it cool till the redness is gone off, and put into it three or four squares of fat bacon; the heat of the shovel will make the fat run and this is to drop over the chicken by way of basting. A great deal of care must be taken in this article; if there be the least foulness on the fire-shovel it will come off with the bacon and black the chicken, or if the shovel be too hot, it will make the bacon run too thin, and burn: the intent is that the heat of the shovel be just enough to let the bacon melt for dripping on the fowl, and when well managed, it gets this way a very peculiar and fine flavour.

Alongside these kitchen paragons were crooked cooks who cheated as much as they felt they could get away with by overcharging or stealing. Tobias Smollet paints the picture of a cook sneaking away from a lodging-house at dawn: 'Her buckets foaming full of our best beer, and her lap was stuffed with a cold tongue, part of a buttock of beef, half a turkey, and a swinging lump of butter.'

Almost the first thing Jane Austen noticed when she arrived at her aunt's in 1801 was 'the exorbitant price of fish: a salmon has been sold at 2s. 9d. per pound the whole fish', more than the basket women who delivered provisions from the market to peoples' homes earned in a month. But as the century progressed, as Bath ceased to be a unique, fashionable spa, the opportunities for milking complacent strangers declined.

Bread prices had been regulated since the 1720s. A century on, the newspapers published weekly the going rate for beef, mutton, veal and pork. In 1833, chickens (smaller than nowadays) cost four to five shillings a couple, ducks slightly less and a goose or turkey between four and eight shillings.

The market too was, in theory, growing more orderly. When the central area was roofed over in 1860, it housed over seventy-five traders, mainly selling greengroceries or fish. Each was equipped with a table, about the size of a school desk, to display his or her wares. With gas lighting, a public WC and running water, it was probably more salubrious than before, but that's not saying much.

Fighting and swearing was routine, despite the presence of a uniformed constable, a clerk and scalesman to check the weights. Drunkenness was also commonplace. Rules regarding public nuisance weren't enforced. Sheepskins from the slaughterhouse at the rear were dragged through the main hall. Now that it was partially enclosed, the stench from freshly killed carcasses sickened many customers.

In the past, only the servant classes would have made their own purchases. The respectable, unfashionable middle-classes preferred to do business in shops where they were served with deference, rather than hobnob with riff-raff.

If you look up at the glass roof today, you can see spokes radiating from the centre as though from the hub of a wheel. It's tempting to suspect that the designers imagined the market at the centre of a city, drawing incomparable raw materials from the surrounding countryside.

Farmers' Market, Green Park.

Locally made cheese at the Farmers' Market.

Instead they devised a constricting gut that the public disliked from the outset.

The city's reputation for good food continued. In 1864, George Cooling created an apple, *Beauty of Bath,* which is still grown today. Ripening very early, in August, it's sharp and juicy freshly picked, but its texture changes rapidly and becomes too woolly to be commercial. Bath tripe and Bath chines (of pork) had their day and vanished from the repertoire. So did Bath polony. The Bath chap (cured pork cheek, coated in breadcrumbs) survives despite attempts by officious politicians to ban it.

Food stalls in the current covered market, so sparse compared to its vibrant counterparts in Spain, France or Italy, barely hint at the role it once played in feeding a population that changed from that of a large village in Queen Anne's day to that of a small city by Queen Victoria's. The descendants of the shopkeepers who did their best to corner the most exclusive produce won, only to lose out to our modern hyper-market culture.

The weekly farmers' market held in the old Green Park Station suggests fleetingly how the city might one day regain its appetite for locally grown produce. It was the first farmers' market to be set up in the country and is thriving as a market that sources food produced in the surrounding countryside, providing a real alternative to supermarkets.

13

GRANDSTAND FINISH

A duel posed a dilemma for gentlemen: it was illegal to fight one. On the other hand refusing a challenge was dishonourable, enough to ruin a reputation. Whether duelling was acceptable, ludicrous or criminal depended on the combatants. When a Widcombe baker (Widcombe was at that time a parish on the edge of town) called out and fought a barber with pistols the *Bath Journal* reported it as a kind of joke; neither came from the right social class. The two encounters between Richard Brinsley Sheridan and Captain Mathews (chapter 14) attracted gossip, but were little more than brawls.

The duel on Claverton Down between Count Rice and Vicomte De Barré in November 1778 sent a frisson of excitement through the Assembly Rooms. It involved high society, gambling, rumour, pathos and, the fondant on the gâteau, a dead Frenchman.

During the Season, everybody played cards. Whist was the most fashionable game. It allowed four people to sit around a table where, depending on the stakes and their skill, winnings and losses were kept within bounds. It had replaced another trick-taking game, loo, which had attracted the high rollers in Nash's era, because pots could swell rapidly and better players who worked out the odds held an advantage.

Lansquenet appealed to the chancers, 'deep players', those whose incomes depended on winning and those who could afford to drop a few hundred pounds in an evening. Like the children's game snap, or blackjack or chemin de fer, success or failure hinged on the dealer's turn of a card. After winning a hand, he could choose: either he passed or he doubled up. A dealer winning six hands on the spin would have turned an original 5-guinea bet into 160.

Jean-Baptiste De Barré (his gravestone in Bathampton Cemetery says he was born in 1749) is a mysterious figure. Accounts of the duel refer to him as Du Barré, Du Bari, de Barre and, improbably, as a relative of Madame Du Barry, mistress of Louis XV of France. The title doesn't signify because Bath overflowed with honorary counts and countesses who had never been ennobled. James Louis Rice (also a 'Count', probably a legitimate one too) was an officer, in one of the

The Royal Crescent where Count Rice and Vicomte De Barré
shared lodgings.

Irish brigades, the so-called 'Wild Geese' Catholic mercenaries who
hired out their services across Europe. The two men were friends, sharing the same lodgings at No. 8 Royal Crescent together with De
Barré's wife and sister.

A few doors away, Colonel Champion lived in a house decorated to
suggest oriental splendour and opulence. An officer in the East India
Company under the governor general, Warren Hastings, whose
impeachment on charges of corruption and mal administration would
become a *cause célèbre*, he was said 'to have enjoyed a good shake of
the pagoda tree'.

Every week, Champion's wife (a picture of her lap dogs perched on
finest Indian silk cushions is in the Holburne Museum) threw an
extravagant party where guests played whist and lansquenet. After one
of these De Barré and Rice fell out over the night's £650 winnings

(more than £70,000 today), about three years' salary for an officer of Rice's rank. The argument simmered for days, but the men remained civil. They had been companions for years and Rice had been part of the family *ménage* for the last three.

De Barré had been suffering from an eye infection that prevented him going out during the daytime. On 17 November at five o'clock, when the valet brought him his medicine in the upstairs salon, he found his master and the captain on good terms. Two hours later the men shared a tureen of soup. Late in the evening the valet was called upon again. An Irishman, O'Toole had joined them. Although they were arguing, the valet thought little of it because he was ordered to prepare a supper for the three of them at one o'clock.

A contemporary pamphlet on duelling claimed to describe how matters came to a head:

> Some dispute arose relative to a gambling transaction, in the course of which Du Barri contradicted an assertion of the other, by saying, 'That is not true!' Count Rice immediately asked him if he knew the very disagreeable meaning of the words he had employed. Du Barri said he was perfectly well aware of their meaning, and that Rice might interpret them just as he pleased. A challenge was immediately given and accepted.

Whether this actually happened, it's impossible to know. Pamphleteers were notoriously free in their rendering of events, but the sequence helps to explain why Rice was found Not Guilty at his trial. According to the established code, the challenger was not considered to be the aggressor.

The three men came downstairs and left the house. Realising what was going down, De Barré's wife ran into the street to stop them. At the inquest the valet stated how he had been obliged to carry her back inside after she had fainted, 'Overcome with terror and fatigue'.

If her reaction seems melodramatic, it's actually quite moderate for the day. Marie Antoinette's lady-in-waiting, Marie-Thérèse Louise de Savoie Carignon, who visited Bath in 1786, staying at No. 1 Royal Crescent, would collapse at the scent of violets or shellfish.

The men, joined by a fourth, one Rogers who was to act as the Vicomte's second, went to the Three Tuns, a coaching inn close to

FALSE COURAGE

Duelling through the eyes of Rowlandson.

the Abbey, where they ordered a coach. Having climbed aboard, they told one of the two postilions to drive to St James' Church, so they could collect a surgeon, and from there to continue in the direction to Claverton Down. Although the surgeon tried to persuade them to wait until daybreak, they persisted, reaching the down about four o'clock.

The modern Bath racecourse lies at the top of Lansdown Hill north of the city. Then the 'two mile course' was located at Claverton. On race days it attracted over 20,000 spectators. The coach bringing them stopped by the grandstand, the duellists and their seconds remaining inside, waiting until dawn, before asking the drivers to take them a little way further, across the course towards Hampton Down near the current site of the university campus. They left the carriage, telling the postilion to await their return.

In his essay on duelling, Jean-Anthelme Brillat-Savarin noted: 'Duels are more frequent in England than France and more cruel since they fight with pistols.' An experienced gambler like De Barré who had trouble with his eyesight must have realised that the odds were stacked against him, that his chances of leaving the ground unscathed were slight.

Unlike the Hollywood version where men stand back-to-back, walk apart, turn and fire, the distance at which the principals stood was regulated by the seconds, in this case at the minimum allowed – fifteen paces. Had the quarrel been over a woman, the challenger would have had the right to shoot first. In this case, though, both men awaited the command 'Allez!'

The anonymous pamphleteer, promising to relate 'details of that black affair and dreadful transaction' gives his version of the critical moments:

The ground having been marked out by the seconds, Du Barri fired first, and wounded his opponent in the thigh. Count Rice then levelled his pistol, and shot Du Barri mortally in the breast. So angry were the combatants, that they refused to desist; both stepped back a few paces, and then rushing forward, discharged their second pistols at each other. Neither shot took effect, and both throwing away their pistols, prepared to finish the sanguinary struggle by the sword. They took their places, and were advancing towards each other, when the Vicomte du Barri suddenly staggered, grew pale, and, falling to the ground, exclaimed, 'Je vous demande ma vie.' (spare my life). His opponent had but just time to answer, that he granted it, when the unfortunate Du Barri turned upon the grass, and expired with a heavy groan.

The details, bar the flourish with the swords, which can be put down to journalistic licence, follow the report at the inquest that took place four days later.

With both men on the ground, their seconds reacted first by examining Rice and fetching the surgeon to him. Next O'Toole examined De Barré although he was clearly dead before removing his watch, his money and a pocket-book he had been carrying. Rogers walked back towards Bath leaving Rice in the surgeon's care. A coach horse was unharnessed and one of the postilions was ordered to ride for help with securing the corpse. Almost immediately he met three labourers on their way to work who agreed to take the dead man to a nearby house.

The postilion then went on towards Bath and caught up with the coach bearing Rice. He had enough presence of mind to ask the postilion to go back to the scene of the duel to collect the weapons. There, he recovered a pair of swords and six pistols, three of which were still loaded. De Barré hadn't been able to fire his second shot. In the middle of the morning, the valet and his other servants recovered their late master.

According to law, someone who fought a duel was liable to be charged with a misdemeanour, with manslaughter or with murder. The coroner's inquest found that the Vicomte De Barré was the victim of manslaughter. Despite this, Rice was charged with murder and sent for trial at the next quarter sessions in Taunton, the county town. Public opinion, though, was on his side. At a performance of Shakespeare's *Henry IV* the actor John Henderson caused a sensation with his rendering of: 'What is honour? A word. What is that word honour? Air, a thin reckoning. Who has it? He that died Wednesday.' Everybody in the audience grasped the reference.

Questioned at the inquest, Rice had insisted upon the fact that the Frenchman had been his closest friend and companion. In the hothouse atmosphere of the city's society where everybody had at least a nodding acquaintance with everyone else, his protestations were believed.

Brillat-Savarin, with typical Gallic cynicism, had remarked that English duelling laws were rarely invoked and almost never applied. Count or Captain Rice was acquitted, despite Mr Baron Hotham, the judge, giving 'an eloquent and pathetic speech on the crime of duelling'. Nor was it the only trial of its kind where, sitting as a Justice, he had to listen to a similar verdict. An Old Bailey jury also found one Cosmo Gordon innocent after a mere ten minutes deliberation.

There the matter might lie except for two teasing loose ends that an Agatha Christie or P.D. James might weave into a plausible mystery. What was the 'gambling transaction' that caused the rift between friends? If they were either sharing their winnings or working together as a team, they were giving themselves a two to one advantage over gamesters playing at the same table.

What kind of an eye problem was De Barré suffering from that prevented him going out by day, but didn't stop him provoking a professional soldier to a fight where he might expect to be at a gross disadvantage? In lansquenet, a dealer, especially one with supposedly poor eyesight playing in a candlelit room, would naturally lean forward close to the table. In this position, he would be in the classic cardsharp's position for palming. In a game where winning hung on the turn of a single card, cheating was child's play.

Perhaps, they were just a pair or successful gamesters. *The New Bath Guide* (1766) catches the subcutaneous cynicism most people felt about gambling:

All other professions are subject to fail
But gaming's a business will ever prevail.

After his acquittal Count Rice left England, returning to the continent to take a small cameo role in the unfolding drama of the French Revolution. Highly regarded by Joseph II of Austria, he was sent to Paris to rescue his sister, Marie-Antoinette, from imprisonment in the Temple. Having prepared a boat to carry the Queen to Ireland where his family had a wine business, he bribed her gaolers to let her escape. At the last moment, she refused the proffered help, only to be guillotined days later.

14

MRS OLIPHANT'S LOVERS

In her biography of the playwright Richard Brinsley Sheridan, Mrs Oliphant, the prolific Victorian authoress, described his elopement with Eliza Linley from No. 9 Royal Crescent as though it were a melodrama, a scene from one of the novels she was so adept at writing. The story had all the elements to keep her lady readers panting in their stays: a beautiful, musical virgin, a quixotic, talented youth, parents who didn't understand their children and a thoroughly bad egg, out to corrupt the heroine. She had at her disposal, the twists and turns of a marriage in France kept secret for a year, lovers reunited with the blessings of parents and, several chapters later, Mrs Sheridan dying beautifully with her husband kneeling at her bedside.

Their drama opened when the Sheridan family arrived in Bath. Thomas, his father, an ex-actor, ex-manager of a Dublin theatre, hoped to set up a school as an elocution teacher, but the notion of an Irishman teaching the English to talk properly touched the satirical nerves of potential students and the venture never materialised.

The Linley family who already lived there enjoyed a unique, but ambiguous position. Thomas, the father, was the city's director of music, a post that left him on the cusp of Society, mixing with it, accepted by gentlefolk but not really one of them. He had at his disposal, however, a special asset – his children. Thomas, a violinist, was a prodigy. The daughters, 'a nest of nightingales', sang and played.

One, Eliza, was a star. Slender, swan necked, with a perfect Greek profile; she attracted men from every age group or shade of social caste. Her voice matched her appearance: 'I have just', eulogised an admirer, 'been to hear Miss Linley sing. I am petrified. My very faculties are annihilated with wonder. My conception could not form such a power of voice, such a melody, such a soft, yet so audible a tone.'

At sixteen, her father had arranged for her to be married to a rich squire already in his sixties. She had balked at the idea. The wedding was called off. Her suitor had made her a tidy present of £3,000 as a goodwill gesture – and a playwright had written a play, *The Maid of Bath*, about the whole debacle.

Sheridan's sisters, Lissy and Betsy, befriended Eliza. His brother Charles was in love with her. As for Richard, Mrs Oliphant believed that his attentions to her were purely chivalrous, quite plausible because at twenty he didn't lack admirers. Sister Lissy adored him:

> His cheeks had the glow of health, his eyes, the finest in the world, the brilliancy of genius as soft and tender as an affectionate heart could render them, the same playful fancy, the same innoxious wit that was shown afterwards in his writings, cheered and delighted the family circle.

Enter Captain Thomas Mathews, married, a womaniser and another family friend of the Linleys. Thirty years on, still living in the city, he resurfaced under the pseudonym of Rattle (as in sabre rattle) to boast:

> There was a time indeed, when I made a figure with the sex and could select from my list of conquests a fair specimen of every degree of rank from the Duchess to the spouse of the squire.

This irresistible force set about turning Eliza into a movable object. He wooed. He persisted. She resisted. She hesitated. Letters were exchanged. She resisted some more. Then, losing her grip on the situation she turned to Richard for advice. They met in a 'mossy grotto' in Sydney Gardens. She confessed to him how this suitor was persecuting her, threatening to kill himself if she wouldn't see him. The meetings were repeated. Our heroine, Mrs Oliphant described, became so distracted, she helped herself to some laudanum of Richard's sister in a botched attempt at suicide. Then Mathews, who had failed to overcome her by pleadings, threatened to carry her off by force.

What could they do? According to Mrs Oliphant 'the two young creatures laid their foolish heads together' (metaphorically speaking) in this crisis of fate – 'the girl thoroughly frightened, the youth full of chivalrous determination' and they decided to elope.

Their elopement was a team effort. Richard's sisters helped with some cash and also with Eliza's packing. On an evening when Mrs Linley was unwell, Richard picked the girl up at her home in Royal Crescent, took her to a hired chaise – the limo of its day – and posted to London. Accompanying them was the wife of a family retainer who travelled as a chaperone, a considerate touch that served to protect

Eliza Linley by Sir Joshua Reynolds, a perfect Greek profile.

Eliza's reputation. Having borrowed some extra funds in town, Richard conveyed his charge across the Channel to the Convent of St Quentin where sister Lissy had passed some of her early childhood.

In Bath, the news of their vanishing act made the *Chronicle*: 'Wednesday evening the elder Miss Linley of this city, celebrated for her musical abilities set off with Mr Sheridan Junior on a matrimonial expedition to Scotland.'

That was only the first shot. Once the rumour machine cranked into action, fuelled as much by a letter that Richard had left citing Mathews as the cause of their escapade, the captain responded by placing an advertisement in the paper rebutting any charge of his own improper behaviour and accusing his rival of being a 'L***' and a 'S********'.

Meanwhile, across the Channel, Richard and Eliza were going

through a secret wedding in a village near Calais, the bride, apparently, returning to the convent after the ceremony. Mrs Oliphant highlights her belief that the marriage remained unconsummated. Years later Mrs Sheridan wrote touchingly to her husband:

> When I left Bath I had not an idea of you but as a friend. It was not your person that gained my affection. No Sheridan, it was that delicacy, that tender passion, that interest you seemed to take in my welfare, that were the motives that induced me to love you.

Whether it did or didn't is something scholars dispute. What's certain is their idyll ended, temporarily at least, when the money ran out.

Eliza returned to her parents. Her father must have welcomed her. She was his chief financial resource. He soon had her singing before George III where 'The king admires… and ogles her as much as he dares to do in so holy a place as an oratorio.'

Richard, lovesick, went back to the bosom of his family and an almighty family row. Mr Sheridan insisted that his son break all contact with the Linleys. His older brother Charles, no doubt jealous too, berated him for his madcap adventure.

Neither of the lovers breathed a word of their marriage.

What happens next is an intended settling of accounts with Captain Mathews. Richard dashes off a letter to the Master of Ceremonies stating that given the public nature of the affront no verbal apology is acceptable and rushes off to London to find and challenge his man. Their encounter in the private room of a tavern, described as a duel, reads more like a bar-room brawl. The men face each other with drawn swords. Richard knocks his adversary's blade aside, grabs his wrist or sword hilt and has the point of his own at Mathews' breast. The seconds step in. The beaten soldier begs for and receives his life. Then, the argument starts as to what form his apology should take. Still exasperated, Richard snaps his enemy's sword. The insult threatens to set them at each other's throats, but he hands Mathews his own sword, promising that details of the fight will not leave the room. Mathews cools down, says he'll never draw on a man who has given him his life.

Of course, the news, with all the circumstances, seeped into Bath Society. Mathews, vexed, challenged Richard again with pistols, prior to swords 'from a conviction that Mr Sheridan would run in on him and an ungentlemanly scuffle probably be the consequence'. Despite this, their second encounter, at Kingsdown between Bath and Bristol, also with swords, proved as messy as its predecessor, with both men rolling on the ground together and Mathews stabbing at Richard with his broken sword tip. Richard, injured, was carried back home. Mathews beat a retreat.

Nobody mentioned the duel to Eliza who was singing in Oxford. Mrs Oliphant says that when she learned that Richard had been wounded she startled those about her by calling out 'My husband! My husband!'. Nobody, apparently, took her distress seriously.

After his recovery, Richard's father took him away from Bath to Waltham, insisting he should put the episode behind him. Through the winter of 1772, he socialised, flirted with other women, apparently leaving Eliza behind. She wrote letters accusing him of inconstancy and affirming her love. The following spring she came to London to sing. They enjoyed secret, Platonic rendezvous until at last the parents got wind of their passion and that Whitsun they married again publicly.

Until then Eliza had been centre stage, the focus of adulation. As soon as they were officially man and wife, she shut down her career in accordance with her husband's wishes. They retired to a cottage in the country 'to enjoy their long-wished for life together'.

Except this isn't quite true because she continued to give private concerts 'for the Nobility' at the home they subsequently set up in Oxford Street when the country life proved too dull for Richard. The diarist Fanny Burney observed that the highest circles of society were attracted to them by the talents, beauty and fashion of Mrs Sheridan. 'Entrance to them was sought not only by all the votaries of musical taste and excellence, but by the leaders of the *ton* and their followers and slaves.'

What was about to change was the meteoric rise of Richard Brinsley Sheridan, dramatist. With *The Rivals*, which drew heavily on autobiographical experience, he composed a play that made his reputation. His earnings from it, together with loans and the help of his father-in-law, allowed him to take on the Drury Lane Theatre. *The Duenna*, an opera, and *School for Scandal*, which used the superficialities of society as its backdrop, set him on a pinnacle while still in his twenties.

His triumphs in the theatre, the career for which he is remembered, paved the way to a seat in Parliament where he was noted for a few histrionic speeches. What altered more was the affect success had upon his personal life. The Romeo persona of his youth never threatened to spill into middle-age. Where Juliet stayed home, or helped with the bookkeeping of Drury Lane, he lived the high life, dissolute, unfaithful, unreliable to associates, friends and even those whom he loved: ironic really, because, Mathews his adversary, passed a scandal-free existence as a Bathonian, his early excesses excused.

When Eliza, still in her thirties, fell ill, she was sent to Bristol, not Bath, to recover. Richard joined her at the end. 'It is impossible for any man to behave with greater tenderness or to feel more on such an occasion', wrote a friend. He stayed at her bedside night and day, overcome with emotion.

Three years after her death, a middle-aged Sheridan remarried, perhaps as means of staving off debts. It was a short-term expedient, because remorse never threatened to transform his habits. He lost his seat in Parliament, a position that had protected him from the debtor's prison. When the Bishop of London visited him on his deathbed, he found bailiffs in the house seizing his effects.

Sheridan by Gilray, no longer the golden boy

Mrs Oliphant's biography of Sheridan has all the force of a cautionary tale, the glorious golden child with high instincts unsupported by strength of character. It's a picture neither more nor less real than any depicted by contemporary academic biographers. What she never mentions but might have is Sir Joshua Reynold's portrait of Eliza as St Cecelia, painted when she was at the height of her beauty. When he was selling whatever possessions he owned to ward off creditors, he kept this until he had nothing left to offer, because it was what he valued most.

15

STRATA SMITH MENDS THE BATH

To posterity William Smith is the father of geology, the man who mapped the geological strata of Great Britain. To the Corporation members who knocked at his door in Trim Street in 1808 he was merely a civil engineer, surveyor and land drainer who had, they knew, been working on the Somerset Coal Canal. Their reason for approaching him was that the flow of water from one of the three springs that were the keys to the city's prosperity was at risk of drying up.

An Oxfordshire blacksmith's son who had left school with a rudimentary education, Smith became an assistant to a Cotswolds surveyor, and was given the responsibility of surveying an estate at Nether Stowey in the south-west corner of Somerset when he was barely out of his teens. Energetic, built like a pugilist, he found fresh employment surveying the route that was being planned for the Somerset Coal Canal in 1793 (see chapter 16). While he was carrying out the work he noted the regular succession of rock strata. He also observed, what had never been formulated before, that different fossils were found in different layers. Sent by the chief engineer, John Rennie, to examine the construction of other canals being built in the Midlands and north of England, he returned to Bath as a senior manager overseeing the canal's building.

While living at Tucking Mill, Midford, he began to colour his map from *The New Improved Bath Guide* that marked five concentric circles from the Abbey, each one representing a mile. What he coloured in with a unique attention to detail were the geological features that he had been studying over the past six years. Effectively, he had entertained himself by producing the first geological map ever. It was to be the prototype for the map of Great Britain that he eventually published in 1815.

While he had been putting the finishing touches to his Bath map, he had also been drawing up a 'table of the Strata near Bath' according to their layers in descending order, starting with chalk and numbered in a continuous series down to coal, the lowest level that was sufficiently known. It was for this work that Smith earned, belatedly, his reputation as one of the principal founders of the science of geology.

Cross Bath (right), Hot Bath (left) and the Hetling Pump Room, today.

Whether he was pushed or fired, he separated from the canal venture in 1799 and instead opened a shop as a land surveyor with a partner in Trim Street. In theory, it was a smart decision because so many of the landed gentry spent part of the year in the city. It also gave him the space to store his collection of over 2,000 fossils, which he was eventually forced to sell to the British Museum for £700 to clear debts he had incurred from an unsuccessful quarrying venture.

From this base, he crisscrossed the country, charging two guineas a day and expenses. He built sea defences in South Wales and on the east coast, drained land on the Woburn estate for the Duke of Bedford, surveyed a canal in Sussex. Not all his work forced him to travel. During heavy flooding in Bath in the winter of 1804, he prevented a landslip on Combe Down by draining off water that had soaked into the clay.

He was also consulted by a speculator, Thomas Walters, who owned the mineral rights to land on the outskirts of the city at Batheaston. Walters had already decided to mine for coal there and may have asked for the surveyor's advice on locating the pit shafts. This association would later return to haunt him.

It's impossible for any visitor to the modern city not to be aware of

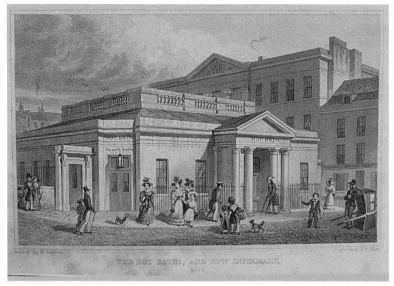

Contemporary engraving of the Hot Bath.

its Pump Room and the hot mineral water from the spring that emerges beneath it in the excavated Roman Baths. He or she may not realise that there are two other springs that also supply thermal waters. One, next to the 'Cube', the new spa building, is under the Hot Bath. The other is under the Cross Baths.

It used to be believed that the source of these thermal waters was somewhere in the Mendip Hills. Rainfall, taking up to 10,000 years to seep through the underlying rock to a depth of about 2 km, is heated to 70°C before resurfacing quickly through a fracture zone or fault beneath the centre of Bath, dropping to 46°C before it emerges. If the 'how' hasn't been challenged, the 'where' has, and geologists now believe that the fissures may lie closer to or under the city.

Although this wasn't known by the Corporation (nor by William Smith), it kept a sharp eye on the amount of water flowing from its springs into the baths and had been doing so since the seventeenth century. The Corporation had also improved the flow to the Hot Bath from 108 tons in 24 hours to 140 tons by engaging the architect, John Wood, the Younger, to build a new stone cylinder to encase the spring supplying it.

The Hot Bath, that was once known as the Lazars', had its own pump room, the Hetling, distinct from what was known as the Grand

Pump Room. Adjacent to the hospital, its waters at that time were a few degrees hotter than those of the King's and Queen's Baths, partly because it was enclosed, partly because it was smaller. When the flow into it threatened to dry up in 1808, the Corporation's committee charged with managing the waters 'hastily sent for' Mr Smith to restore the flow to the Hot Bath and the Hetling.

Against opposition, he obtained permission to open up the spring, which meant undermining the expensive work that had been carried out a generation earlier.

Having dug down to the level where the spring water should have been bubbling up to the surface, he realised that it had started flowing into a new channel. During the work carried out to restore it, the temperature was so hot and steamy that the tallow candles of the navvies melted. Having diverted the stream back to its original course and repaired the 'leakage under the Lepers' bath', Smith was able to increase the rate at which the baths filled.

The diagnosis and resolution of the problem had taken about three months. The Corporation, delighted with his work and his previous efforts to stop a large swathe of Combe Down sliding down into the valley, engaged him to carry out running repairs at the King's Bath and the Cross Bath, where the reduction in the rate at which the respective springs filled the baths was also causing concern.

Meanwhile, the Batheaston coal-mine project had been going badly. There is no evidence that Smith had advised Walters that he would find coal there. However, he is known to have told another company who wanted to explore an area near Bruton about thirty miles away that they would not, thus saving its investors considerable expense.

The main concern for the Bath mine was the shaft itself, which kept filling with water that had to be pumped away through an adit. When the shaft had been dug and lined to a depth of about 300 feet, the prospectors had sunk a borehole several hundred feet deeper, causing what Smith described as a 'cataract' of thermal water to rise up through the shaft. He wondered whether there could be a link between the water that was gushing out of his mineshaft and the reduction in the amount of water that was feeding the Cross Bath.

To control the water at the mine, Walters had been pumping it out six days a week, with the engine switched off on Sundays. Over a six-week period Smith cross-checked the rate at which the bath filled when the Batheaston pump was working against the rate on the Sunday when it wasn't. *The New Guide Through Bath* for 1811 reported the filling had fluctuated from sixteen to twenty-eight hours. This was enough to convince a large chunk of popular opinion that the miners were inadvertently siphoning off waters from the baths.

In actual fact, the report had been inaccurate, since Smith had observed a significant but inconclusive spread of sixteen to eighteen hours.

This still placed him in an awkward position, one in which he faced a conflict of interests. He was advising the would-be colliery owner on the one hand, while committed to help preserve the hot springs that were probably being depleted as a result of the drilling. It was a dilemma that resolved itself, because the following year the cost of pumping the water from the shaft had become prohibitive and Walters decided that he would be throwing away capital if he were to continue the exploration.

Looking for a scapegoat, he sought to shift the blame for his failure on Smith, arguing that the surveyor had encouraged him to continue mining years after he had realised that striking coal was improbable. When winding up the company Walters further implied negligence, stating that his geologist had been too busy working on his 'Report on the Strata of Great Britain', his map, to pay a visit to the site.

The consequence of the pit's closure for the springs was that, probably on Smith's recommendation, the pit was back filled and sealed. How he might have resolved his divided loyalties is hard to tell, but he had proposed to the Corporation that they should pull down the elegant structure that housed the Cross Bath before he would be able to proceed. This controversial measure would have kept the Corporation arguing long enough for him to distance himself from a project that ceased to be necessary once the shafts stopped disgorging water.

At the largest, King's Bath, the fault was less with the spring that filled it than the way it had been tapped. Unlike a swimming-bath, it wasn't paved, but its bottom was a mixture of mud, sand and gravel. The cylinder through which the water rose needed bedding in more solidly. This meant emptying the water and digging down to the base of the cylinder through which it rose so that this could be properly anchored.

One of the workmen recorded how much the baths had needed a makeover: 'There was a large body of sand in the King's Bath... which fell in on the spring as the water was pumped out and a quantity of the brass railings fell in after.'

William Smith left Bath in 1813 to complete the finishing touches on his famous map. He wasn't, though, about to be fêted as the trailblazer he undoubtedly was. The professional jealousies of academics in a newly formed Geological Society prevented his map from gaining the recognition it received after his death. In his private life, he was bankrupted, spent time in a debtor's jail and was unfortunate enough to marry a nymphomaniac who ended up in a lunatic asylum.

Where antiquarians of his day, however, were talking about the myths of Bladud and the physicians were inventing stories about the miraculous healing powers of Bath's thermal waters, William Smith knew what they were and how to preserve them.

From the *Geological* magazine, 1869
Centenary of William Smith's Birth

Bath can claim that the first collection of fossils stratigraphically arranged was made by Smith whilst at Cottage Crescent. The first table of the strata was dictated by Smith at Pulteney Street. The first geological map was coloured by him whilst living near Bath. The first announcement of the publication of a geological map was his prospectus, dated from Midford. The first introduction of his discovery to the public was through the friends he made in Bath.

16

JANE AUSTEN WALKS TO THE CASSOON

Among the more dramatic moments of Jane Austen's private life was the trial of her maternal aunt, accused of shoplifting ribbons. While on remand at Ilchester jail, she and her husband, James Leigh-Perrot, had enjoyed the privilege of staying with its governor because they were considered respectable gentlefolk. The winter they spent under lock and key did little for James' gout. His wife, another Jane, was acquitted at the Spring Assizes of 1800, but she would have faced transportation to Australia had she been found guilty.

The year before the trial, Jane Austen had stayed in Bath with her mother and brother for the first time. Even at that time she had found her uncle hobbling around the town, hiring chairs for the shortest of journeys. However, he seems to have recovered, because he was spry and able to accompany her for morning strolls around the city when the Austens stayed at his home in the Paragon in 1801. In a letter to her

An open stretch of the South Somerset Coal Canal.

sister Cassandra soon after her arrival she noted: 'My uncle has quite got the better of his lameness, or at least his walking stick is the only remains of it. He and I are to take the long planned walk to the cassoon.'

What was this mysterious 'cassoon'? Where was it?

The term itself was a popular deformation of caisson, a gigantic watertight coffin fitting tightly into a large cistern that, filled with water, was used for raising and lowering canal boats in lieu of locks.

Canal fever was at its height when Jane moved to Bath. The Kennet & Avon that would eventually link the River Avon to the Thames was more than half completed. On her first outing Jane records strolling along a recently finished stretch of the canal by night, perhaps where it passes through Sydney Gardens, which was close to her relations' home.

The cassoon, though, was something of a completely different order. It belonged to the South Somersetshire Coal Canal. Begun a little later than the Kennet & Avon, and routed to link with it near Monkton Combe, the canal was seen as a means of transporting coal from the Radstock coalfield to Bath, because it had been cheaper until then to import coal from South Wales across the Bristol Channel than from the mines on its doorstep, which used packhorses or horse and cart to carry the loads over difficult terrain.

Jane and her uncle's planned destination wasn't a triumph of cutting-edge technology. They were anticipating a close-up look at an engineering folly that had been entertaining Bath's citizens with its ups and downs for almost as long as the 'Cube' has preoccupied its contemporaries. Had it succeeded, as it initially seemed to, it would have been a wonder of the waterways world, rather than a stone-lined hole in the ground, all that remained of the project when they saw it.

The canal's line followed the course of a brook, the Cam, running through a valley from Paulton to the junction with the Kennet & Avon. The engineers did their sums, measured a fall of forty metres and decided that they would need to build a flight of twenty-two locks at Combe Hay, a hamlet lying about four miles south of Bath.

However, having studied the latest technology – an experimental caisson designed by Robert Weldon – they changed their minds. He had constructed a half-size version, the only one of its kind, on the Ketley Canal in Shropshire. They gambled that this was a modern solution that could move barges faster and more cheaply. The decision

The Kennet & Avon Canal behind Sydney Gardens.

made, they set about constructing the first of three intended caissons, or cassoons, completing it in 1798 two years after advertising in the *Bath Herald* for masons to build it.

To walk there and back wasn't such an extraordinary feat for Jane who was accustomed to country rambles. Not long after the anticipated outing with her uncle she describes a similar promenade with a Miss Chamberlayne to the village of Weston:

> It would have amused you to see our progress. We went up by Sion Hill, and returned across the fields. In climbing a hill Mrs. Chamberlayne is very capital; I could with difficulty keep pace with her, yet would not flinch for the world. On plain ground I was quite her equal. And so we posted away under a fine hot sun, she without any parasol or any shade to her hat, stopping for nothing, and crossing the churchyard at Weston with as much expedition as if we were afraid of being buried alive. After seeing what she is equal to, I cannot help feeling a regard for her.

How her middle-aged relative coped with the steady, uphill slog along the Fosse Way (though it's possible that they would have taken the longer scenic route, skirting Ralph Allen's Prior Park and on to the canal site via Midford Castle) we may only guess. That's a mighty long way to go to examine a hole, and maybe, assuming that work on a second cassoon had started before being suspended, a partly finished hole.

Actually they would have had more to interest them. The canal building was still going forward. As a stopgap response to the problem of transferring cargo with no means of moving it by boat, the company's navvies would have been labouring on an inclined plane system that would open that autumn, whereby coal could be shuttled downhill. Cranes would hoist it from the barges into wagons that when full rolled down a gentle 300-yard slope, at the same time acting as pulleys to haul empty wagons uphill.

This clumsy system that involved repeated loading and offloading would end once the locks that were part of the earliest plan had been completed. Had the caisson / cassoon performed as intended it would clearly have been a more productive solution.

To imagine how it worked, think of a large box, not floating but immersed like a submarine in a water tank with two doors, one near its top, the other at the bottom.

The objective was to float a canal boat on one level through the

The view Jane Austen might have had of Bath when she arrived with her family.

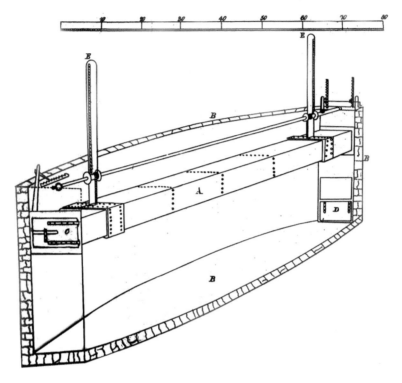

Cross section of the cassoon. The barge went into the long box running through the middle.

entrance, into the box, seal it, raise or lower it to the other level and let it out.

This ingenious contrivance consists of a wood cistern, having two square apertures with a slide door to each, at the respective levels of the upper and lower Canals; In this reservoir (being always full of water) is immersed a Caisson, or hollow vessel; having a door water-tight at each end, for the purpose of receiving and enclosing a boat; this Caisson is ballasted, to be specifically of the same gravity as water, consequently will descend or ascend in its surrounding medium (with or without a load) with the greatest facility. Each end of the Caisson, when brought in contact with the square apertures of the reservoir, is also water-tight; this is accomplished by an inverted valve, discharging the water from the space between the slide-door of the reservoir and the door of the Caisson, the pressure instantly then fixes the Caisson to the apertures, therefore the slide-door may be opened with much ease, and of course that of the Caisson. The boat may then be received for ascension, the doors re-shut, and the great difficulty of releasing the Caisson from the aperture (against which it was so power-fully pressed) obviated, by opening another valve to refill the space just mentioned; it consequently follows, the pressure on the Caisson will be as before, equal on all its sides – by discharging a small quantity of water from the Caisson by means of a cock into the lower Canal, it becomes lighter, and instantly ascends to the upper aperture; the same process with the valves completes the design which is truly philosophical.

From the *Bath Herald*, 27 June 1795

The hydrostatic theory was faultless. In practice, too, after the odd glitch, the caisson delivered. In seven minutes a long boat could enter and exit the 66-foot deep tank. During its maiden test-drive a bolt sheared off and the attempt was aborted. It was repaired and series of faultless runs took place between summer 1798 and spring 1799. These culminated in a major public relations coup when the Prince Regent watched a demonstration. Twelve days later sixty gentlefolk enjoyed a pleasure ride that would have given them a thrill on a par with the early Montgolfier balloons that occasionally entertained Bath society.

The euphoria was short-lived. That May the South Somersetshire Coal Canal's management committee was aboard a boat inside the caisson when it got stuck. They escaped, but not before they had nearly suffocated. The accident convinced them to abandon their experiment and write off its losses. Ostensibly, they claimed that the caisson was already four times over its £1,200 budget and that repairs would put an extra £1,000 on the bill. More likely they were reacting to their own near-death experience.

There are two not incompatible explanations for what had gone wrong. Although the cistern sides were barrel shaped, the caisson matched its length. If they had been built of limestone (Bath stone) rather than impervious bricks, the walls could have swelled, causing the jam.

Alternatively, if the tank was emptied at any time for repairs, groundwater in the surrounding earth, Fuller's Clay that soaks up moisture, could have forced the structure inwards.

The royal visit, the pleasure ride, the accident with its dramatic outcome, had all happened within a month of Jane Austen's earlier arrival in the city. They occurred when, on most days, as she confided in her correspondence to her sister Cassandra, her uncle was unable to move. Perhaps the roots of their 'long planned walk' date from the conversations they had then. In any event, she enjoyed his company more than her aunt's, shoplifter or no.

The demise of the prototype submarine didn't prevent the canal's opening. The 'inclined plane' acted as a final link between the upper reach at Paulton and a shorter stretch past the village of Monkton Combe where it joined the Kennet & Avon at Dundas aqueduct (a piece of this is all that survives). Like many commercial waterways, it did eventually reward its investors. In 1858, for example, it carried 165,000 tons of coal, twenty-two barge-loads per day. Typically, it fell into decline and was finally abandoned, although the Great Western Railway opened a branch line in Edwardian times that followed much of its course.

For a piece of engineering on a scale to warrant royal patronage, the cassoon's exact location has proved difficult to trace. It has given its name to a field and a house. Its remains, allegedly, lie beneath a certain horse chestnut. Industrial archeologists have, without managing to solve the conundrum, consulted maps, dug trenches. The exact spot was already contested by the 1870s. A monograph 'Rambles About Bath' supports the 'conker' tree theory, refuting another claim that a flagpole opposite Caisson House marked it.

Currently, the best guess is that the remains may lie alongside the dismantled Pump House, which housed a steam engine needed to circulate water through the locks, although excavations here haven't upported this theory.

Locks, planes, engine house, cassoons and a railway that marked the canal's line, which cut through and scarred a picturesque valley, have been reclaimed by nature. All that's left of the canal are a few overgrown bridges and ruined lock gates. The coal mines that fuelled Bath's hearths have gone too, their presence merely signalled by the pyramid slag-heaps of Radstock. This may not be such a bad thing.

The valley at Monkton Combe through which the canal used to run.

The soot from the city's fires was already helping to tarnish the walls of its crescents when Jane Austen lived there. With her dislike of the city's smog and vapours, she would probably approve of their disappearance from the landscape.

17

BECKFORD'S SALE

In 1801, William Beckford, described by Byron as 'England's wealthiest son', decided to pull down his family pile, Fonthill Splendens in Wiltshire, and hold a sale. William Wyatt Dimond, manager of Bath's Theatre Royal, bought his 'state bed of crimson velvet, together with accompanying chairs, sofas and curtains adorned with burnished gold... and borrowed by George III to sleep in'.

Beckford no longer needed the mansion his father had built. He was replacing it with an abbey, a Gothic skyscraper of a palace, the ideal toy for an eccentric mega-rich gentleman with a passion for collecting *objets d'art*. To most of the country's aristocracy, who had ostracised him for his pederasty, he was thought to be a recluse. That hadn't stopped him laying on a grand festivity for Lord Nelson and his mistress, Lady Emma Hamilton, as a house-warming party for his extravagant folly.

By 1823, he had grown bored with his plaything. It was too cavernous, too draughty. Nor was he the nation's top plutocrat. A combination of bad and fraudulent management had decimated the revenue from his Jamaican sugar plantations, the inherited basis of his fortune. The moment had come for another sale, probably the sale of the century. William Hazlitt, who viewed the auction, damned it with as good a hatchet job as was ever penned by an art critic:

> Mr. Beckford has undoubtedly shown himself an industrious bijoutier [jeweller], a prodigious virtuoso, an accomplished patron of unproductive labour, an enthusiastic collector of expensive trifles – the only proof of taste (to our thinking) he has shown in this collection is his getting rid of it.

Years later, when he had established himself at his new home in Bath (1822), Beckford implicitly agreed with this verdict, claiming that much of what was auctioned had been introduced by the auctioneers and had never belonged to him.

His move to two houses on the ends of Lansdown Place West and Lansdown Crescent, which he connected by a flying gallery that

William Beckford's house at the corner of Lansdown Crescent, with the flying gallery.

served as a part of his library may have been a pioneering example of downsizing, but he hadn't lost his taste for creating follies or collecting. On top of Lansdown Hill, he built himself a 150-foot tower topped with a belvedere from which he could survey the Bristol Channel to the west. He might have enjoyed a view of Fonthill Abbey twenty miles to the east, now the property of a gunpowder merchant, except that the tower collapsed three years after Beckford had sold it. When he set about furnishing his new and more durable tower, he called upon a local Milsom Street auction house, English & Becks. Public auctions had been one of the amusements of fashionable society: auctioneers, with constant access to furnishings and fittings, extended their businesses to handle interior decorating. Despite the earnings from their money-no-object patron, English & Becks went bust, resurfaced as English & Fasana and, in 1841, three years before Beckford's death, English & Son. Father and son, both named Edmund, had a good working relationship with the old connoisseur, not least because he never haggled over prices and paid cash.

Another string to the auctioneers' bow was funerals. Beckford, into his eighties, died in 1844. On behalf of his daughter, Susan Euphemia, Duchess of Hamilton, his sole legatee, English & Son, organised his funeral with the kind of pomp and circumstance of which he would have approved, with 20, 000 onlookers lining the streets to the Abbey's cemetery where he was entombed in a pink granite sarcophagus.

The next year and again in 1848, English & Son continued their lucrative association with the Beckford estate, holding two auctions, 'one of the Tower's effects, the other of his houses'.

Except for objects of sentimental value, which the Duchess kept for herself, they were handling the prized possessions of one of the greatest art collectors of his day. Aged fifteen Beckford had published and been paid for a mock-serious *Biographical Memoirs of Extraordinary Painters,* composed for his Fonthill housekeeper. They included the lives of Blunderbussiana, son of a Dalmatian bandit, and Sucrewasser of Vienna. This early facetiousness contrasted with his obsessive, discerning approach to collecting in later life. Today, twenty pictures he owned are in the National Gallery, among them a Raphael, a Perugino and a Bellini.

In both sales, however, third-rate artworks and copies of great artists that were passed on as originals were mixed in with the extreme opulence of Beckford-owned possessions and his passion for Old Masters. In an age that had little conception of provenance, the Englishes were able to pad out the sales with dozens of lots that had no connection to the collector.

It was a scam that those in the trade connived at, as a poem about the Fonthill auction showed:

> When gems, bronzes and paintings are gleaming half shown
> Mr Beckford's we mean, sir – (t'other half wouldn't please sir)
> From tables of ebony, rosewood and one
> Which they tell us belonged to the Prince of Borghese, sir,
> But geese we should be all we hear thus to hug
> Since we know they may come from the Prince of Humbug.

Ironically, Beckford had understood the problem of faking that bedevilled the art world. Showing a guest round his Lansdown property, he had drawn his attention to a Canaletto, remarking: 'Very few of those attributed to him are really genuine, but of mine there can be no doubt as this painting and several others that I have were got directly from the artist himself by means of the English consul at Venice.'

In his prime, he had an excellent sense of a picture's commercial worth. He paid more for a pair of Claudes than any other landscape paintings purchased in the eighteenth century and almost doubled his money inside four years when he sold them for £10,500. In 1947, when Christie's auctioned them, they fetched £5,300, a loss in real terms of over 90 per cent but today they might have a value in millions.

Lots 334–336, according to English & Son, were 'the very last things that Mr Beckford ordered and saw them on his deathbed'. Religious subjects, they were painted by an up-and-coming painter in Bath called Willes Maddox. Known as 'lunettes' from their half-moon

One of the mysterious demi-lunes.

Beckford's Tower on Lansdown Hill.

Interior of Beckford's Tower.

shape, their late owner had wanted to hang them in a part of the tower known as the Sanctuary, an alcove where he had placed a statue of his adopted patron saint, Anthony of Padua.

What was odd about them, was their number. Only three were auctioned, but a complete set of four has since been discovered.

Several sales catalogues have survived. Notes scribbled on them show how much bidders were prepared to pay for the serendipitous mixture of high art and doubtful tat, sometimes who bought what, occasionally a quick sepia sketch of an 'object of vertu', a spontaneous impression (Velasquez – 'a bad copy'; 'positively ugly'; 'very elegant'; 'very awkward') and verbatim quotes of the auctioneer's technique: '150 are bid, five are offered, 155, may I say 60. I shall say 60. I won't repeat it. Yes 60 bid for you, sir. May I say five – 70, down it goes, no stop there's another bidding, just in time'.

The Sale of the Tower lasted four days, of Lansdown Crescent, where a Poussin fetched £750 and a 'Titian' five guineas, three more. Their combined income should have given a serious boost to the English & Son profit and loss account. Instead it was the prelude to a scandal.

Edmund snr had been bankrupted before. His father's will, which left him only ten pounds for mourning, stated: 'It is my intention that all sums he may owe me at my death on bond or note shall be paid to my executors. And I give my son Edmund English no further of my property', a clear implication that his parent had already bailed him out of debt.

But by 1852, when he was over seventy, when he had become a respected pillar of respectable society, he and his son vanished.

They had planned their disappearance carefully. The father had managed a week's start, having left the city, ostensibly to make arrangements for a picture sale. His son had announced that he was going to Wales to a house he was furnishing and leaving instructions for work to be sent on to him.

Where they went is a mystery. 'Why' was known almost immediately. Despite their reputation for being among Bath's leading traders, 'as upholsterers and masters of artistic effects in household effects they had a reputation second to none', their firm had been operating at a loss, not just in the short term, but for years. They had extended their credit to breaking point and from there they had turned to forging signatures on promissory notes in order to lay their hands on cash.

Once their absence from Bath became conspicuous, a creditor filed against them in the Bristol District Bankruptcy Court and their fraud was uncovered. Bailiffs immediately seized their furniture, but recovered nothing of the thousands with which they had decamped. Nor did this include the firm's £20,000 business debts, enough to fill a gallery with Rembrants and Raphaels.

Other than a journalist's guess that they had fled the country, that was the last that was heard of them. Edmund jnr's wife was left destitute with four children, living with her sister-in-law. In an attempt to raise some funds for her family she printed a circular appealing for charitable assistance. In it she complained that her own private fortune had been unsecured and 'was sacrificed in the lamentable transactions of the firm'. Having made her cry for help she swiftly died of cancer.

The story of the Beckford sales and their aftermath has a twist. Remember the missing 'lunette'? It is unlikely that the Duchess had taken it. Nor had Willes Maddox recovered it as a souvenir or in lieu of an unpaid bill for his architectural paintings of the tower; he died in Turkey in 1853.

The three paintings listed in the sale catalogue depicted *The Temptation in the Wilderness, Christ's Agony in the Garden* and *The Annunciation*. The fourth, *St Anne and St Mary*, was not mentioned. Nothing is known about the subsequent whereabouts of all the pictures until 1933, when they were bequeathed, as a quartet, to Bitterley church in Shropshire by Colonel Price Wood of Henley Hall. They hung there unrecognised until an antique dealer doing a routine valuation in 2003 recognised the artist's work and made the connection with the tower. From there, they were sent to a Dorchester saleroom and bought by the Beckford Tower Trust for £16,000. Restored, they will hang in the spot for which they had been intended. A comment in the 1845 catalogue margin had described them as 'Germanic', odd companions in the Sanctuary for Beckford's favourite Portuguese St Anthony, who chose to be a Franciscan friar rather than lead the life of a wealthy nobleman for which he had been destined, a wry antithesis to Beckford's own life of aesthetic self-indulgence.

His treasures, like exotic flotsam, still appear in salerooms around the globe, passed like currency among rich collectors, or snapped up by museums. A set of gilt spoons and pieces of china from the sales that were bought by another rich Bath dilettante, Sir William Holburne, are displayed in the Holburne Museum. Cabinets of Beckford's own design, which he would have commissioned English & Son to have made for him, fetch fortunes when they appear on the international art market.

As William Hazlitt noted, Beckford collected 'the difficult, the exclusive, the unattainable in profusion', as only a man who could afford anything might. Everything went under the hammer, knocked down by a crooked auctioneer. And who knows, perhaps the same thing is happening to these choice baubles still?

18

BLACK RIBBON
OR BETTY COBBE AND THE HUNTINGDON CONNEXION

Bath has more than its share of ghosts: the suicidal 'grey lady' who haunts the Theatre Royal; the naked Roman soldier; the white-haired man who haunts the gravel walk in Victoria Park; 'Tiny' the ghost of Beckford's dog buried at the Tower; and 'Bunty' the barmaid at the Beehive.

It has had a few bloodstained incidents too, ones that ought to be enough to raise the dead, such as the murder of Maria Bagnall in Marlborough Buildings by a manservant called Richard Gilham. To hide the fact that he had been robbing his mistress, he had bludgeoned and cut the throat of the girl, then pretended that she had been attacked by a burglar. Unfortunately for him, stolen property was found at lodgings he had rented: he confessed, was convicted and hanged.

Lady Betty Cobbe's ghost was not from Bath, but arrived with her when she and her husband, Thomas, set up house in Bath, in Marlborough Buildings, to escape the rising costs of maintaining a large estate outside Dublin. Their life in Ireland had involved plenty of socialising and entertaining, so it was to be expected that in Bath a wide circle of acquaintances soon knew the tale of a phantom bed-side visitation that she must have repeated often at tea parties or over dinner.

It had a reliable family pedigree to support it. Betty, as a girl, had composed her own romanticised narrative. The story's real heroine was Nicola Sophia, her grandmother, but on the principle of Chinese whispers, the story was soon doing the rounds as 'Betty Cobbe's ghost'.

As the story goes, when Nicola and her cousin John Le Poer, the 2nd Earl of Tyrone, were young they had decided after an argument about the existence of an afterlife that whoever died first would return, if able, to convince the other that there was a spirit life beyond the grave.

After her marriage to Sir Tristram Beresford, Nicola saw little of her cousin. One morning she came down to breakfast looking drawn and wearing a black ribbon around her wrist. Sir Tristram, noticing his wife's appearance, inquired what was the matter. She refused to give an explanation, instead asking whether any letter had been delivered because she was expecting one that would announce the death of the Earl of Tyrone. Her husband's response was along the lines of 'Don't be ridiculous.' She, however, continued to insist that her cousin had passed over at four o'clock on the previous Tuesday.

On cue, a letter from the earl's steward was delivered that echoed in every detail the information she had given.

To add to the effect she had created, she stated: 'I am with child and it's going to be a boy.' This prophecy was fulfilled.

From the morning of her disclosure to her husband's death, Nicola continued wearing the black ribbon and did not divulge what it was concealing. After a period of mourning, she remarried the officer son of friends, to whom she bore three children. His dissolute behaviour forced her to seek a separation from him. However, he returned begging her forgiveness and promising that he was a reformed man. They began living together again and she bore him another child. Having recovered from her confinement, she invited her adult son and daughter by her marriage to Sir Tristram to pay her a visit, together with the Archbishop of Dublin and an old clergyman who had christened her.

In the course of the house party, Nicola was talking to the clergyman: 'Did you know that it's my forty-eighth birthday today?'

'Actually,' the priest answered 'you're only forty-seven, for your mother had a dispute with me once on the very subject of your age, and I in consequence sent for and consulted the registry, and can most confidently assert that you are only forty-seven this day.'

Rather than being pleased with the news she blurted out, 'You have signed my death-warrant. Leave me. I haven't much longer to live, but have to settle something important before I die. Send my son and my daughter to me immediately.'

When they came to her, she began telling them of her early friendship with her cousin, and of the bargain they had struck: 'One night, years after this interchange of promises, I was sleeping with your father at Gill Hall, when I suddenly awoke and discovered Lord Tyrone sitting visibly by the side of the bed. I screamed out, and vainly endeavoured to rouse Sir Tristram. "Tell me," I said, "Lord Tyrone, why and wherefore are you here at this time of the night?"'

The spectre reminded her of their agreement, gave her the hour and date of his death and the news that she was pregnant. Nicola, quite resourcefully in the circumstances, asked her late cousin to prove that he wasn't part of a dream. He wafted up the bed hangings and pushed them through a metal hook in a way that was impossible for anyone to do in their sleep. Still to be convinced, she let the spirit sign his signature in her pocketbook. Finally she asked for tangible, irrefutable proof of his presence. He laid his hands 'cold as marble' on her wrist; the sinews shrunk up, the nerves withered. 'Now,' the ghost said, 'let no mortal eye, while you live, ever see that wrist', and vanished.

When she rose the next morning she fetched a broom and untwisted the bed hangings before binding a black ribbon around her wrist that she had worn until the present moment.

Then she revealed to her children the ghost's parting shot: she would die on her forty-seventh birthday. An hour later she died. The children removed the ribbon to discover a withered wrist impressed with a black mark exactly as their mother had described. As proof of the authenticity of the story Lady Betty Cobbe had both her ancestor's pocketbook and the black ribbon. She may well have worn it herself to heighten the impact of her Gothic legend.

What is clear, though, is that she grew tired of relating the history. Queen Charlotte, George III's wife who was visiting Bath, asked her through the intermediary of a lady-in-waiting for the truth of what had happened. Lady Betty in a sniffy reply: 'presented her compliments, but was sure the Queen of England would not pry into the private affairs of her subjects, and had no intention of gratifying the impertinent curiosity of a Lady-in-Waiting'.

Another reason for her apparent distaste could be that in Bath she discovered Methodism. It's ironic then that the story of this conversion should have its own paranormal spin.

The first cousin of Lady Betty's husband was Selina Hastings (née Cobbe), who married the Earl of Huntingdon, and was also the mother of Lady Moira his sister-in-law and a second daughter, also called Selina. This Countess of Huntingdon, immensely rich, widowed in early middle-age, was central to the Nonconformist revival led by the Wesleys and George Whitfield. She used her wealth and influence to encourage the upper classes to lead better lives. Because she could afford to she hired a stable of private chaplains and built a select network of chapels.

The first of these outside London was in Bath, where she based herself. Nominally, it belonged to the orthodox Anglican religion, but because it included living accommodation for a priestly appointee, it operated outside the jurisdiction of the local diocese.

Self-righteous, she preached a doctrine of personal salvation. Her biographer, Dame Edith Sitwell, wrote of her:

> No matter what her company, she would insist on the conversation being turned upon religion, the terrible sins of those present, the hopelessness of their future state as compared with hers, her own former sinfulness and present righteousness, her virtue in contrast to her companions' lack of virtue, and other matters of the same kind.

It was a message that converted plenty of fun-loving aristocrats, even after she died, her Irish cousin among them, so that when Lady Betty could be prevailed upon to tell her ghost story, she gave it a moral twist. Nicola Sophia and the Earl of Tyrone had been brought up by heretical deists who didn't believe in the Bible's revelations. When the earl's spirit came to haunt his cousin, it was because he had been permitted to do so in order to confirm the truth of the Christian gospels.

If Betty Cobbe's ghost lost something of its edge after it became an apology for faith, the mysterious dreams of the Countess of Huntingdon's daughter were never properly explained. Lady Moira, who was close to her sister, dreamed that Selina sat down at her bedside and spoke to her saying: 'My dear sister, I am dying of fever. They will not tell you of it because of your situation [Moira was pregnant] but I shall die and the account will be brought to your husband by a letter in which the handwriting has been disguised.' On waking, she recounted her dream to her governess, Moth. Days later the letter breaking the news of Selina's death written by her brother in disguised handwriting arrived.

Allowing for the resonance between the two accounts, it would be tempting for a sceptic to claim that the earlier could have inspired the later one. However, Lady Moira is recorded as having at least two more premonitory dreams, the first warning her of the death of her second son with whom she had quarrelled and the other on the night before her remaining son unexpectedly died. Moth, the governess, appeared in both of these warning dreams, but she had 'crossed over' many years earlier.

Betty Cobbe's spectre became one of the most popular Regency fables, retold by, among others, the novelist and poet Sir Walter Scott. We only have a record of Lady Moira's phantasms thanks to a manuscript written by the Reverend Henry Cobbe, which was recovered by a noted feminist, Frances Power Cobbe, who was herself the great-granddaughter of Lady Betty.

Frances' agnostic approach to parapsychology is the no-nonsense one that might be expected from a toughened spinster who worked at the roughest edges of Victorian society: 'I do not disbelieve ghosts; but unfortunately I have never been able comfortably to believe in any particular ghost-story.'

Her incredulity about the supernatural, contrasts with the nice little anecdote that she told about her ancestor:

> Lady Betty was a famous compounder of simples and of things that were not simple, and a 'Chilblain Plaister' which bore her name was not many years ago still to be procured in the chemists' shops in Bath. I fear her prescriptions were not always of so unambitious a kind as this. One day she stopped a man on the road and asked his name – 'Ah then, my lady' was the reply, 'don't you remember me? Why, I am the husband of the woman your ladyship gave the medicine to and she died the next day. Long life to your ladyship!'

19

WHATEVER LOLA WANTS

'Whatever Lola wants, Lola gets
And little man, little Lola wants you.'
Cole Porter

Lola Montez, siren, harpy, courtesan, royal mistress and Spanish dancer, was never what she seemed. When she spoke to journalists, she invented what they wanted to hear, knew what would make a good story. When she wrote her memoirs or had them ghostwritten, she mythologised every aspect of her life, lying about her birth, her family, her husband, her amours. She manipulated, or tried to, everyone with whom she came into contact. Her public behaviour wrote the rulebook for future divas. She threw tantrums, horsewhipped gendarmes, was as compelling in a law court defending herself as on stage dancing the tarantella.

Dead at forty, she had seduced individuals and audiences across the world from Sydney to New Orleans. Her relationship with King Ludwig of Bavaria had brought about his abdication. Her bigamous marriage to a baronet had kept London gossip columnists on the edge of their seats. She had captivated Franz Liszt, the composer and virtuoso, who called her 'The most perfect, the most enchanting creature I have ever known.' Photographers snapped her alongside an Indian chief. All true stories. Tales of her enjoining a lover to stab the winner of a card game for attempting to receive payment, or betting with a highwayman for his pistol, of befriending Spanish bandits are just a sample of many anecdotes invented about her, often by herself.

Everywhere she went she created a sensation, except in Bath where, incidentally, she lived longer than anywhere else. That was because she spent five years here, a slip of a girl at a private boarding-school. Even so, she managed to leave the city in a way that gave more than a hint of the *femme fatale* in the making.

On her first visit to London as Lola Montez, she told a half-credulous reporter that she had learned to speak English from an Irish nurse during a seven-month sojourn in Bath. It was a suitable fiction for a woman whose 'black eyes, taper ankles and... clear olive complexion' epitomised the Anglo-Saxon notions of Andalusian beauty. In fact, Eliza Rosanna Gilbert, born County Sligo in February 1821, owed her looks to the Emerald Isle.

Her mother, illegitimate, apprenticed to a Cork milliner, had married a junior officer, Ensign Gilbert in the East India Company's army while he was home on extended leave and she was a 'very pretty'

Lola Montez at the height of her fame.

fifteen-year-old. They returned to India where almost immediately the soldier died of cholera on a boat trip upstream from Calcutta. A widow of limited means Mrs Gilbert didn't hang about. Within twelve months she had married Lieutenant Patrick Craigie, a Scot. The future Lola thought her mother vain and trivial. She was probably not too concerned about parental responsibilities because she sent her only daughter back to Scotland to live with her husband's relatives when the child was five.

Fostered by her step-aunt and uncle, Mr and Mrs Rae, Eliza moved south of the border with them when they set up a small school in Durham. However, her parents (5,000 miles away) decided that she should be educated as a lady. They approached Captain Craigie's (he was climbing the ranks to become, eventually, adjutant-general of Bengal) former commanding officer, Major-General Jasper Nicolls, who had retired to Reading with a fistful of daughters, in the hope that he would find her a boarding-school appropriate to her station. Like many other ex-colonials, he opted to send her, still only eleven, to the spa.

An art master who had taught Eliza during her time with the Raes depicts her as a clever, capricious, seductive Lolita:

Eliza Gilbert (of the intermediate name 'Rosanna' I knew, or at least remember, nothing) was at that time a very elegant and beautiful child of about ten or (perhaps) eleven; of stature rather promising to be tall than actually such for her age, but symmetrically formed, with a flowing graceful carriage, the charm of which was only lessened by an air of confident self-complacency – I might almost say of haughty ease – in full accordance with the habitual expression of her else beautiful countenance, namely, that of indomitable self-will – a quality which I believe had manifested itself from early infancy. Her features were regular, but capable of great and rapid changes of expression. Her complexion was orientally dark, but transparently clear; her eyes were of deep blue, and, as I distinctly remember, of excessive beauty, although bright with less indication of the gentle and tender affections of her sex than of more stormy and passionate excitements. The mouth, too, had a singularly set character, far more allied to the determined than the voluptuous, and, altogether it was impossible to look at her for many minutes without feeling convinced that she was made up of very wayward and troublesome elements.

Camden Place in which Eliza's boarding school was situated.

The general's choice of academy, in Camden Place (now Camden Crescent) typified the kind of establishment designed to finish girls in preparation for advantageous marriages. Managed by two sisters, Eliza and Caroline Aldridge, its primary role would have been 'the mental improvement and moral habits and domestic comforts of the pupils'. This translates roughly as teaching them to read, behave in company and become a conventional nest maker. It was, however, unusual in that the fifteen academicians who learnt dancing, sewing, drawing, piano and Latin, spoke French through the week and were only allowed, officially, to converse in English on Sundays. Anyone caught breaking the rule was fined.

How this regime affected Eliza we can't be sure, except that she always spoke French, though fluently, with an Anglo accent. She did claim to have visited Paris with Mrs Nicolls, but there were sides to her character that made her an unsuitable companion for the general's daughters. The major-general in his diary referred to her as a 'dirty whelp'. Even Mr Grant, who had taught her the rudiments of art, had to admit she could be difficult:

Camden Arms above the doors in Camden Place.

The violence and obstinacy, indeed, of her temper gave too frequent cause of painful anxiety to her good kind aunt; and I remember, upon one occasion it was necessary, before Eliza could receive her lesson, to release her from solitary durance, in which she had been kept all the previous part of the day for some rebellious outbreak of passion. The door was opened, and out came the incipient Lola Montes, looking like a little tigress just escaped from one den to another!

Of her education, given her future career, dancing would have appealed to her, though country dances such as the Basket of Oysters, the Trip to the Pavement and the New Pump Room might have seemed tame by comparison with her on-stage performances. They would, though, have given her an opportunity to touch hands with members of the opposite sex. In her unreliable memoirs she recalled clandestine tête-à-têtes with a pubescent Sir F— in the lanes behind the crescent, small beer by comparison with what happened when Mrs Craigie returned to see her nearly grown-up daughter.

She came to collect and accompany her back to the subcontinent where she had lined up a potential husband of the right sort. On her journey to England that had taken the better part of a year, she had befriended a Lieutenant Thomas James, a fellow Irishman. During the voyage she had explained the purpose of her visit, suggesting that he should call on her in Bath where she intended renting lodgings until the end of the school year.

The meeting between Mrs Craigie and Eliza after a decade's separation showed that the older, still physically attractive parent lacked both sense and sensibility. When the child rushed to embrace her she apparently reacted by commenting: 'Oh my dear child, how badly your hair is dressed.'

Eliza moved into the accommodation her mother had rented, but continued attending her classes. Then Mrs Craigie's 'cavalier' showed up – thirtyish, average height, brown hair, blue eyes and, according to Lola, white teeth. He was allegedly engaged to be married, but showed no inclination of separating himself from his shipboard companion. Daily he rendered her the service of walking her daughter to Camden Place. He continued this escort duty for weeks until finally he proposed to Eliza that they should run away together to Ireland and be married. The idea must have appealed to a girl who had lived in the city from which Richard Brinsley Sheridan eloped with another Eliza – Eliza Linley. Retrospectively, she alleged that she expected this not quite dashing soldier 'To love her like Papa'. Apparently, they had travelled less than thirty miles before he was 'no longer my Papa'.

True to his word, though, he did carry her to Ireland where they were married by his brother John, priest of the parish of Rathbeggan, County Meath.

Major-General Nicoll's reaction to the 'wretch Gilbert' was typically charitable. 'I always predicted the vanity and lies of Eliza Gilbert would bring her to shame and she has started badly, if not worse, for leaving school in June, she married a company officer without a penny.'

With the benefit of hindsight Lola might have agreed: 'Runaway matches', she once admitted, 'like runaway horses are almost sure to end in a smash up.'

The immediate consequence of her wildness was, ironically, that she had to return to India. Rather than sharing a cabin with her mama, she had to endure a voyage with a snoring husband who clung to her like a boa constrictor. Her attempts at settling into the life of a memsahib were half-hearted. She was soon aboard another ship heading back to England, apparently to mend her health after falling off a horse.

It was on this trip that she met George Lennox, a lord's son her own age. Their adulterous behaviour in the cramped conditions on board, in contrast to her mother's discretion with regard to Thomas James, scandalised fellow passengers. Those who tried to remonstrate with Mrs James were invited to mind their own business. On landing, she and Lennox lived together until the landlady discovered their liaison and turfed her out.

Once the news reached Lieutenant James in Bengal, he successfully sued for divorce. After the decree had gone through with its attendant publicity, Mrs James's behaviour had stripped her of any possibility of respectability. She was twenty-one, with no means of support other than some cash sent her by her stepfather.

The fate that awaited her as a remorseful woman who had lost her reputation had she been still in Bath was the Penitentiary in Walcot Street. It provided a refuge for 'the girl who falls through her love under the promise of marriage and the girl who has been brought up in immoral surroundings... the idle girl fond of fine dresses and frivolous amusements and the wilfully depraved'. There, after training, she might have made a good servant, a housekeeper or even a governess.

Instead, she went to Spain returning to London with a new identity – Dolores Montez, widow of Don Diego Leon. Her cover lasted just long enough for her to give her triumphant opening performance, before she was outed as the ex-Mrs James, but it was the name that stuck to her. She never returned to Bath, but the city was no longer the capital of revelry, scandal and gossip it had once been, which meant it was not the place to welcome a divorcee, however gay.

CRAIGIE'S TOAST

Patrick Craigie, Eliza's stepfather, enjoyed a small reputation
for this recipe, which appeared in the Reform Club's
recipe book by 'Mrs Mills'.

Craigie's Toast will commend itself to those who wish for a quickly made dish. Allow one egg and a small tomato to each person. Beat up the eggs and add the tomatoes minced, also seasoning – a few capers or a little gherkin finely chopped is very good – and a little milk, ketchup and water, or diluted extract – half a teacupful to 4 eggs. Melt a good piece of butter in saucepan, pour in the other ingredients, and mix over the fire till thoroughly hot. Cover, and allow to cook by the side of the fire for a few minutes, then serve piled up on crisp toasted S.W. Biscuits, a kind of square rusk, probably made with oatmeal.

20

CHAIRS AND CHAIRS

Wheels on chairs weren't a new idea when they hit fashionable Bath. As long ago as the sixteenth century a Nuremburg carpenter, Balthazar Hachal, invented a multifunctional one that doubled as a commode. The French had devised a two-wheeled *brouette*, a prototype people's wheelbarrow guaranteed to shake anyone going up the Rue du Faubourg St Honoré half to death, as well as a *vinaigrette* that was pulled like a trap.

In eighteenth-century England any gentleman who read the *Gentleman's Magazine* would have been familiar with the gouty chair whether or not he had seen the real thing in action. It was an elegant Chippendale front-wheel drive. Handles on the armrests turned the axles that joined to the wheel bases. Indoors, it may have kept invalids off their toes but about town, it didn't solve the problem of getting from the parades to the pump rooms.

For that, they already had a choice. If they were going for treatment at the baths, small closed chairs or *bayes* were the favoured transport. Boxes, hung between poles, carried by two porters, they had their strong points. They provided a room-to-room service. So long as the stairs were wide enough to negotiate, chairmen fetched and carried their charges in insulated comfort.

Those who lived in town, who could afford to pay the wages, owned elegantly finished sedan chairs to take them

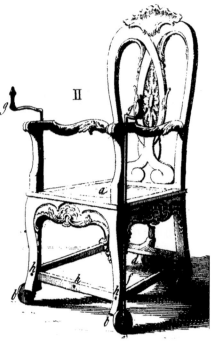

Gouty chair

on their round of social calls. Licensed 'chairs', like taxis, were all-weather, robust, no-fuss conveyances. They were a part of any urban town-scape. London had 300; Bath at its peak had 200.

It's likely that the earliest wheeled Bath chairs were adapted from these. One survived at Hampton Court until Edwardian times when the palace was used for grace-and-favour residents. Elderly dowagers were towed along its corridors in wicker-seated chairs, and also propelled in an antique 'push', a sedan chair on wheels. A photograph of a similar contraption with two large rear wheels and two smaller front ones, 'blitzed' during the Second World War air raids, is in

Sedan chair

Bath's archives. It's a kind of 'coachlet', drawn by manpower.

Because he is the first recorded maker of Bath wheelchairs, James Heath has been credited with their invention. Since his business last-ed right through the Regency, competing with a coach-builder and harness maker E. & H. Vezely and a 'wheel chair maker' John Dawson, he or his rivals probably changed the design to the elongat-ed three-wheeler with an optional cabriolet hood that became, with modifications, the characteristic shape up to its demise.

Although it couldn't negotiate a staircase, the Bath wheelchair had the prime advantage over bayes of halving the labour cost. A second benefit was its ability to carry invalids where horse-drawn chaises, coaches and cabriolets were not permitted, to the Spring Gardens, for instance or along the walks.

A luxury Bath chair designed for the Great Exhibition of 1851.

It was also allowed indoors, as Dickens described in *Pickwick Papers*:

There is another pump room [the Hetling], into which infirm ladies and gentlemen are wheeled, in such an astonishing variety of chairs and chaises, that any adventurous individual who goes in with the regular number of toes, is in imminent danger of coming out without them.

Sedan chairmen had been licensed since 1708, their fares regulated by distance, measured from specific landmarks. In mid-century, six old pence would take a passenger 500 yards, one shilling a mile, roughly from the Abbey to the Assembly Rooms and back. Disputes over excess charging were referred to an alderman.

Chairmen could be fined or dismissed for a range of offences, such as drunkenness (a perennial complaint), fighting (common), swearing (routine), refusal to carry a fare, insulting passengers or unserviceable vehicles.

The faults were not always on their side. Chairs were vandalised to the extent that they had to form their own watch committee for protection.

One, belonging to John Pike and Samuel Tyly was attacked several times, the interior lining torn out and the cushion and cushion cloth stolen. Seven chairs parked in Bartlett Street near the Upper Assembly Rooms were cut and defaced, so angering the body of chairmen that they stumped up a £20 reward for information leading to a conviction.

In 1792, during the French Revolution's Reign of Terror, when fears of republicanism in England were at their height, 326 chairmen signed a loyalist petition stating: 'We are conscious that our livelihood and the happiness of ourselves and families depends entirely on the prosperity and peace of the kingdom in general and the city in particular.'

Having proved themselves to be patriotic citizens, they called a wildcat strike the following year so as to be able to increase prices, claiming that they were having to charge the same rate for carting their fares up the steep Bathwick and Lansdown Hills, where many of the new houses were being built, as on the level. On licensing day, they marched as a body to the Guildhall, abused the mayor, trashed the chairs of blackleg colleagues, and refused to carry passengers.

The response to their demonstration was immediate. The Corporation set up a committee to consider their grievances, and caved in.

A Sedan chair and Bath chair outside the Pump Room.

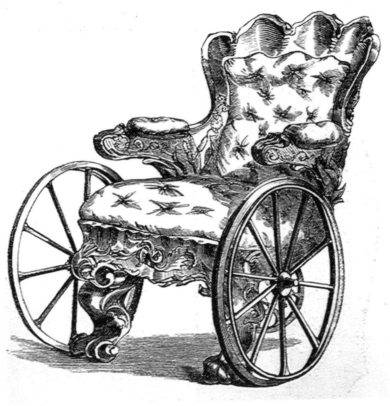

From gouty chair to Bath chair to wheelchair.

Chairmen could charge a fare of sixpence for each 300 yards of hilly and 500 yards of level ground.

By-laws, still in force at the time of the Battle of Waterloo (1815), fined chairmen thirteen shillings and four pence if they failed to operate without paying their licences, but fare dodgers were sent to prison for a month. Despite their previous successful direct action, charges had barely risen during the sedan era. A shilling would buy 1,173 yards instead of one mile, but a passenger could keep his chair waiting ten minutes on a sixpenny journey for no extra charge.

The change from the sedan to the Bath wheelchair happened gradually through the first half of the nineteenth century as a consequence of the shifting nature of the city's visitors. From a fashionable place of entertainment that promised cures for the unwell, the spa was turning into a medical centre that existed primarily to treat the sick. Many of the licensed chairmen owned both wheelchairs and sedans, one to carry people to the baths or the pump, the other to social engagements. Once the partying stopped and the numbers of elderly patients in town increased, sedans, which had always needed two carriers, went out of vogue.

By now the Bath chair had taken its characteristic form. An adaptation of the earlier design, it protected its sick passengers against fresh air, by enclosing their lower body in a wooden chassis and protecting their upper with a window. Later models, bought by individuals for their personal use, were often open.

The firm that James Heath had founded flourished into the Victorian period, moving from its original Bennett Street location near the Circus to No. 6 Broad Street. At the Crystal Palace Exhibition in 1851 it scored a major coup when Prince Albert guided the Empress of France to a prize-exhibit Bath chair, designed like a Chesterfield on wheels, when she complained of fatigue. She commented upon its comfort and the Prince Consort immediately bought it for her as a gift.

This was a plush, beautifully upholstered machine worthy of royalty, but already the chair's reputation was attracting the black humour that made it the butt of 'sick' jokes. A 'Reverend X' posted the following advertisement in the *Chronicle* in November 1863:

> The clergyman of a town parish in which there are several crippled persons at present unable to attend divine worship will feel grateful to any gentleman or lady who will give him an old Bath chair for the use of these poor people; two blind men having offered in this case charitably to convey their crippled neighbours to the house of God.

In the social pecking order, a career as a chairman rated one notch above that of a common labourer. Once in the job, it represented work for life. For instance a Mr George Owen, born in Thatcham in 1831, went to Bath, turned chairman in 1856 and continued pulling until his death, aged sixty.

His job had changed subtly from the more fashionable days. He and over 150 others – sometimes a licence was shared by two or more chairmen – worked off twenty-two fixed ranks set during the sedan era. But, instead of the narrow circuit around the centre, he might expect to pull customers up the hills of an expanding city more frequently. His fares paid more. They carried shopping with them and no longer wore ball gowns. Chairs would shuttle the elderly around amenities such as Victoria Park, created from the old city's common and opened by the Queen when she was still a princess. Instead of dominating the pavements with cries of 'Give way!', chairmen were expected to show respect to pedestrians.

Having established themselves as an ideal transport for the infirm, Bath chairs also spread to other spas, to Buxton and Harrogate, where two unladylike Battenburg princesses raced each other aboard chairs down Parliament Street after a visit to the Turkish baths. Their exuberance contrasted with the image of the chair that identified it with sickness and decay. By the early-twentieth century it epitomised the geriatric nature of Bath inhabitants:

> We were often told in the Army that the speed of a squadron was the speed of its slowest horse; similarly the speed of Bath is that of its slowest chair. Some months ago the local paper reported that a woman was run over by a Bath chair… but from my slight knowledge of Bath I imagine that the injured person and the pusher of the chair were probably sleep-walking at the time of the collision. That is the great danger here. As long as you can keep awake you may survive.

Apart from killing numbers of chairmen, the Great War consigned Bath chairs to the role of ferrying convalescent and / or mutilated soldiers. By then it was already apparent that automobiles would put an end to their usefulness. Attempts were made to bring them up to speed. One firm designed a self-propelling version; another one with a two-stroke petrol engine that bowled along at twelve miles per hour. They lingered on in seaside towns as curiosities, occasionally pulled by donkeys. The actor Robert Morley remembers riding in one as a boy growing up in Folkestone:

> 'I think,' the doctor would say, soon after the spots disappeared, the rash faded, the temperature subsided, 'I think he could go out for a little, in a Bath chair.' And in a bath chair I went. The very best

CHAIRS AND CHAIRS

Folkestone Bath chairs had folding mahogany shutters with windows through which one looked out on to the patient back of the attendant, silently plodding ahead. With the shutters drawn one was insulated from the noise, a silent world with the delicious uncertainty that one might have suddenly become stone deaf.

In Bath, the numbers of chairmen dwindled to a handful. Some were still drunks; one fell into the Avon and drowned. Asked whether it was possible to earn a crust, a stoic chairman replied: 'We don't. We do a little carpet-beating now and then and odd jobs. It isn't much of a life.'

The last man standing, a veteran of the Somerset Regiment, Ernest Ball, kept going through the Second World War, spending days outside the Pump Room, often without anyone hiring him. He said his chair, its leather upholstery beautifully sprung, its floor carpeted, its wheels bound with vulcanised rubber, was a hundred years old. Throughout its history, it had been inspected regularly by the chief constable and the chairman of the watch committee to ensure that it was in good repair.

The best thing about the demise of the Bath chair is that it's final. Not even the most optimistic entrepreneur hoping to make a fortune from tourism would consider reintroducing it. Black, slow, heavy, it was a cumbersome form of moving those who were unable to shift for themselves. The sedan chairs were more fun and avoided the association with an invalid chair. They carried glamorous Cinderellas to their princes. The chairmen might go to the wrong address and the fare could end up at a party with strangers. And there was always the risk that one of the men would trip over his heels and the chair would end upside down in the gutter!

21

FIZZY POP

Corn Street, Milk Street, Avon Street: the names don't trip off the lips of guides showing visitors around the city. Until postwar planners decided to tear out their bomb-damaged or neglected housing and workshops by the roots, replacing them with a college and a coach / car park, the location of these streeets was a rotten-toothed area of the old city. Lacking the glamour of the uptown Georgian showpiece architecture, it had few to defend it. Never pretty or salubrious, it had been, in the second half of the nineteenth century, with its shops, its bars, its ragged school, exclusively working-class.

Just north of the Avon, contemporary visitors were advised to avoid it: 'On the low lying lands on the bank of the river to the West, there is a region of filth, squalor and demoralisation where poverty and crime lurk in miserable companionship.'

Police constables thought twice before making an arrest here. Petty crime flourished. When they weren't pitching headfirst into the polluted water, the street urchins were barracking the Salvation Army band. It was here in 1872 that Johnathon Burdett Bowler, brass founder and engineer, set up his business. The first half of his job description is how he advertised himself in the local directory, the second represents him for what he was, a skilled manual worker capable of turning his hand to most any mechanical task, whether fitting a new lock or repairing a water closet.

Around Bath, he enjoyed a small reputation. His father had been landlord of a tavern, the Bell in Rivers Street. After his fathers's death, when Bowler was still an apprentice in a foundry, he took on the role of supporting his siblings as well as his own growing family. He left the foundry as a foreman, having found time to freelance his way round the city on a velocipede, altering leg irons for a surgical instrument maker, repairing gas fittings and doing jobs for employers as disparate as a pony-carriage operator and a dentist.

With what remained of his leisure hours, he reared pigs and sold vegetables from a smallholding. He also bought and rented out five properties.

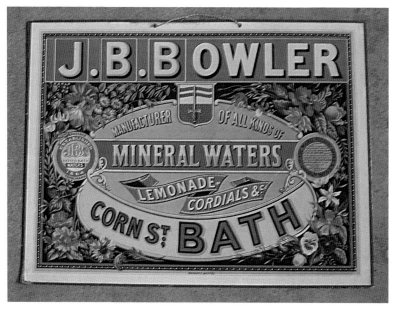

Bowler used mineral water in his drinks, but not the waters from the spa!

Once he became self-employed he turned his hand to any mechanical task that came his way: he had made soda-water apparatus for a Bristol firm and a pump and bottling plant for Brooks, an 'aerated water' manufacturer in Bath. This was no budding Coca Cola or Schweppes, but merely one of several small businesses making Seltzer, ginger beer and fizzy pop, the same as could be found in almost every town in the country. He must have satisfied his customers because he received a further order for making soda-water machinery from a Bristol firm.

This may have been the equipment he bought back in 1874 from Hopkins in Bristol for £4.5.0 because he had decided to go into mineral water for himself. The city had been exporting bottled water, its health-giving, sulphurous hot spring 'waters', since Beau Nash's day. The great man had made money shipping it around the country. Mr Bowler was not looking beyond the H_2O that came out of the tap.

The trick of carbonating water ('impregnating water with fixed air') had been developed by the cleric Joseph Priestley a century earlier as part of the research that led to his discovery of oxygen. Using chalk,

Bowler was one of at least five fizzy drinks makers in the city.

water and oil of vitriol he managed with the aid of a bladder to press the air it released through a tube into a water-filled bottle standing inverted in a basin of water. 'If this discovery', he wrote in the preface to the pamphlet describing his method, '(though it doth not deserve the name) be of any use to my countrymen and mankind at large I shall have my reward.'

Coincidentally, it was while working for the Marquis of Lansdown as his librarian, at Bowater House ten miles from Bath, one year after publishing this paper that he made the discovery of oxygen for which chemists remember him.

Priestley had conjectured that his 'pregnant' water had medicinal properties and suggested mixing it with lemon, salt and wormwood as a treatment for a sore throat, a visionary anticipation of the tonic waters that would later become popular.

'Pop', the familiar English name for fizzy soft drinks had been current for half a century when Bowler opened his manufactory. It had been coined to describe the noise when the cork was drawn from the bottle. By his day, though, technological improvements had taken place to prevent accidental blowouts.

Nine of his thirteen children were girls and three of these, Annie, Fanny and Louisa, managed the day-to-day running of his soda business, leaving him free to deal with other aspects of 'engineering', either constructing mineral-water machinery for export to the United States, or inventing a 'copper and gunmetal cylinder' on a condenser, or fitting a central-heating system, or engraving a brass plate for a solicitor's front door, or repairing a garden gate.

The basis of all the sweetened soft drinks was a mixture called Twaddle, the same word that has since come to mean nonsense. Its recipe, 112lb sugar, 4oz saccharine, 50 gallons water has in the old imperial system of measurement a certain elegance: four quarters of a hundredweight, four ounces, 400 pints. This sugar syrup was flavoured with essential oils such as lemon for lemonade, or vaguely medicinal compounds as in 'Quinine tonic', or a cocktail of ingredients in Bowler's Bath Punch.

Conditions were hard, especially for the bosses. Bowler arrived at 7 a.m. and left at 9.15 p.m. His daughters worked elbow to elbow with the four employed hands. They wore wooden clogs because the floor was awash, as well as rubber aprons and face masks intended to protect them from shattering glass bottles. This precaution was evidently insufficient because Louisa lost her sight in one eye.

A contemporary account of life on the shop floor describes how deft mechanics could be at removing shards and shavings:

> In all workshops the men frequently get small chippings of iron, or some other material with which they are working, into their eyes, and when this happens they at once go to one of their mates, who, seeing what has occurred, places the patient with his face to the light, turns up the top eyelid – on the inside of which any particle of cold matter that enters and remains in the eye is almost certain to be found; with his penknife or 'scriber' he then takes off the irritating substance. Many mechanics – but more especially stonemasons, and that class of engineers technically known as 'fitters' – attain a remarkable degree of proficiency in cleaning eyes in this manner.

After Louisa's accident, a protective grille was fitted, but by then the damage had been done.

Fanny and Annie measured the essences, prepared the twaddle and labelled the bottles. The process of carbonating the water wasn't much more complex than Priestley's experimental method. The gas, produced by the action of sulphuric acid on crushed marble, was stored in a gasometer until needed, ready to be pumped into the water once the bottles were filled. If these exploded, it was because their mass production was in its infancy and many were flawed. Before the modern stopper designed to withstand pressure was invented, 'pop' makers relied on Cobb bottles containing a glass bobble, which rose to the neck, acting as a seal. These were popular with children who would break the bottles to get at them for their games of marbles. Bowler had the idea of rewarding them with two glass balls for every bottle returned intact so that he could recycle them.

Business around the city was brisk in summer, slow in winter. He had regular contracts for his ginger beer with the Radstock coal mines. The Blathwayt Arms, close to Lansdown racecourse, placed large orders for race days. Competition, in an age before national brands, was stiff. His was one of eight suppliers in 1878. Roundsmen, who delivered for him, weren't the robust six-foot tall draymen employed by the large breweries. Having passed from pub to inn to tavern during the

Early soda siphon in the Museum of Bath at Work.

day with their charge of soft drinks, they often relied on their horse to bring them back to the factory in one piece. One quick-witted roundsman who was hijacked, threw his takings into the cases of empties and escaped by whipping his horse to a gallop.

That day payment had been in cash, but the preserved Bowler accounts show it was often in kind – a goose, or a joint of pork or, on one occasion, an offer to paint Mr Bowler's portrait.

In winter, his horses were stabled on the firm's premises. Their manure was piled into a dung heap that, fermenting, acted as a kind of primitive biomass central heating (the only heating) for part of the factory. The 'gaffer' didn't believe in mollycoddling his men or his daughters, telling them that artificial heating was something for people with soft bodies and weak characters.

Neither he, nor his family, nor his employees signed the pledge, but he had a strong vested interest in the success of the Temperance Movement, which had a strong foothold in Bath. The local chapter's president was Isaac Pitman, inventor of shorthand. Whether by chance or design, the year Bowler began manufacturing had coincided with the Licensing Act that curbed the hours that public houses could sell liquor. The names he chose for his beverages, Orange Champagne, Cherry Ciderette, or Horehound Beer smack of the same worthy ideals as our modern vegetarian sausages and mince.

For the extreme prohibitionists, those who blamed the demon drink as the root of working-class vices and the pledge-takers, ex-Lushingtons who had seen the light, pop was wholesome and health giving. Fanny would not have made the link between the twaddle she had been tasting and the pair of false teeth her father bought her (on the business) in 1899.

After their father's death in 1911, twelve of his thirteen children turned the business into a limited company, persisting with his policy of diversification, which was no bad thing because the days of the small independent soft-drinks supplier were numbered. Although the company continued making soda water until the firm closed in 1969, by 1920 they had opened a motor garage, were repairing bicycles and undertaking maintenance for factories and businesses, such as laundries, across the city. One way or another, most of the population of Bath that had needed something fixing would have had dealings either directly or indirectly with J.B. Bowler.

Only one of his thirty grandchildren, Ernest, took an interest in the family firm, letting it drift until 1969 when the council slapped a compulsory purchase order on the building in order to bulldoze it.

That ought to have drawn a line under the Bowler history. It didn't, not quite because Bowler had an almost obsessive need to hang on to things, never throwing away anything that might one day have a use. It was a trait he passed down through his genes. He, or rather they, kept the most unlikely items as stock: calendars for giving away to customers, several hundred blue light bulbs, ladies' skirt-lifting tongs to avoid dirtying the hems of their dresses. No longer making soft drinks, the firm had left the factory exactly as it had been on the last day of production.

A Bath businessman, Russell Frears, was so fascinated by the time capsule he saw that he bought the factory's contents, paperwork (including orders written on the back of wallpaper or sandpaper sheets), bottling plant, tongs, and all for £2,000. Having founded the Bath Industrial Heritage Fund to preserve them, he had the factory interior photographed so that he could duplicate it at a new location.

The site he chose, Camden Works, an old pin factory that had been a real tennis-court in Georgian times, became the Museum of Bath at Work. In a city that trades so heavily on its more distant past, the higgledy-piggledy jetsam of the late-industrial age has a serendipitous effect. In the area of the museum devoted to the factory, the deafening rattle of bottles that one-eyed Louisa would have lived with so long she had ceased to notice, almost makes you want to walk out almost as soon as you have gone through the door. Once the ears have adjusted, however, it's not hard to imagine what it was like to be slithering through water and broken glass back in 1900.

22

SWEDENBORG TO *WALLACE AND GROMIT*

Armed with a Gladstone bagful of diplomas from the National Art Training School (afterwards the Royal College of Art), a thirty-year-old teacher from North Shields, William Harbutt, assumed the post of headmaster at the Bath School of Art and Design in 1874.

The Georgian city where he planned to settle had lost some of its lustre. Its honey-coloured crescents and squares had been dusted a sooty charcoal grey by a century of coal fires. Neither the Season nor the Company existed as before. Instead, as a prosperous provincial town, it had settled into a demure middle-age, still dependent on its mineral waters and the incomes of invalids who tapped into them.

It had also, in a substantial way, reinvented itself as a sober seat of learning. George Allen's Palladian mansion, Prior Park, had become a Catholic seminary and college. Kingswood, the school that the founder of Methodism, John Wesley, had opened near Bristol, had been relocated to a new site on Lansdown Hill. The Royal School (where Lola Montez would certainly have been educated had she been born twenty years later) turned the daughters of army officers into young ladies.

The new headmaster was joining a state-funded school that had been set up after the Great Exhibition of 1851 as a reaction to the perceived shortage of artistically motivated designers urgently needed to support manufacturing industries.

Born the son of a Tyneside galvaniser, by temperament a sculptor, the job probably suited him. He was both ambitious and idealistic, so much so that after three years he resigned his headship when the management committee turned down his plans to expand the school.

Cut adrift, newly wed to a fellow teacher, he freelanced in Bath until he had raised enough funds to open his own Paragon Art Studio where he taught clay modelling and painting.

His wife Bessie was a talented miniaturist, who had been commissioned by Queen Victoria to paint portraits of her and her late husband, Prince Albert. Had she gone on working the Harbutts might have earned a comfortable living in the town, but she was fully engaged raising their six children – a seventh died in infancy. The couple took in lodgers to help pay the bills.

When money grew even tighter, Harbutt considered emigrating to Australia, going as far as applying for a post as drawing master at a school in Melbourne.

Like many Victorians, he held deep religious convictions. Instead of channelling them through one of the mainstream denominations or one of the many Nonconformist chapels, he had joined the Bath New Church Society that followed the religio-philosophy of Emanuele Swedenborg.

An eighteenth-century theistic scientist, Swedenborg had tried to pinpoint the location of the human soul. Initially he had decided that it wasn't concealed anywhere in the brain. However, a series of dreams and waking visions or hallucinations convinced him that Reason was in touch with a distinct spiritual dimension in a universe that, as he now viewed it, was an amalgam of layered experiences either physical or mental or spiritual, one where actual objects corresponded to intellectual or psychic states.

His far-from-orthodox ideas appealed to artistic temperaments. For example, the symbolism which William Blake adopted in his poems ('Tiger! Tiger! burning bright' and 'Jerusalem') linked directly to the Swedish enthusiast.

Swedenborg believed, and the New Church Society that grew from his doctrines developed his theme, that the Bible was written in a language of hidden correspondences that pointed to Good and Evil.

'Clay', for instance, in an Old Testament quotation: 'Woe to him… that ladeth himself with clay', is not desirable. However, in 'Now, Jehovah… we are the clay, and Thou our potter; and we all are the work of Thy hand' it certainly is.

The notion of 'improving' modelling clay, that dried too soon, that his young art students found too claggy, heavy and hard to fashion must have appealed to Harbutt, because he would have seen it as a means of doing God's work. By rendering it more supple, more malleable, easier to mould, he would have felt that he was reducing its grosser qualities. Modellers would be able to focus more readily on the higher, faculties of creativity, of imagination.

Working in the basement of an address in Alfred Street that he was renting, Harbutt concocted the basic recipe, composed of clay, chalk, fatty acids and petroleum jelly that he would later name Plasticine.

From pastry-sized batches that he gave to his nine- and eleven-year-old sons to play with – they made flowerpots and soldiers – he graduated to small-scale production.

At the back of the house, he flattened slabs of his clay dough on a board with a garden roller, leaving it for weeks to ripen. He shaped it into grey blocks with the paddles that cooks used for butter pats.

From the outset he realised his clay had a commercial value, ironic because the school he had come to Bath to lead had aimed to promote the partnership of art and industry. And he was to show as much aptitude in business as he had as an educator.

The teacher in him recognised the advantages of his discovery in the studio, but the parent realised its wider appeal to the very young: 'The child', he said, 'could obtain his box of water colours, crayons, pencils at a penny, but nothing to satisfy his modelling instincts.'

The name Plasticine that had itself resulted from a family brainstorming was registered as a trademark just as the twentieth century was breaking. Harbutt offered a red, blue and yellow pack for sale, paid an artist friend to design the box cover and wrote a six-penny booklet: 'How to use Plasticine as a home amusement for children.'

He spent his first £5 advertising budget with *The Royal Magazine*.

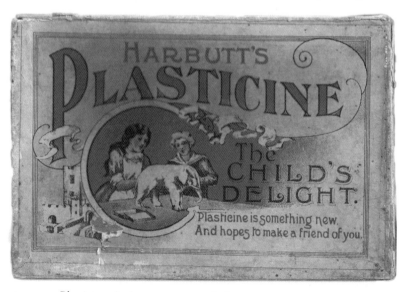

Plasticine elephants, a century before Creature Comforts.

BATH CURIOSITIES

It had a circulation of around one million readers who paid their monthly three pence for the latest stories by Baroness 'Scarlet Pimpernel' Orckzy and Sax 'Fu Man Chu' Rohmer. His slogan: 'Plasticine is something new, and hopes to make a friend of you' caught the public imagination.

To meet demand he moved out of his workshop at 22 Milsom Street into an old mill at Bathampton close to the Great Western Railway and the Kennet & Avon Canal. From there Plasticine went around the world. In Bath, his faith made him, for his day, a benevolent employer who might close down a production line in summer for a works' cricket match or, in winter, so his staff could go ice-skating on the canal.

In keeping with his patriarchal status and bushy white beard, he was given to grand Swedenborgian pronouncements: 'He who follows is always behind.' He never drank alcohol. He opposed vaccination. He was an anti-vivisectionist.

During the First World War two very different uses were found for Plasticine. Harbutt's sent boxes of it to shell-shocked soldiers convalescing from the trenches as a means of therapy, but in 1917 the firm's chief modeller, Albert Blanchard, also built a model of the German positions on Vimy Ridge in Flanders for the British Army ahead of its assault.

Blanchard once wrote of Plasticine: 'You can roll it, cut, mould and shape and then crush up what you've made and start all over again.' That wasn't true of the thousands of lives lost in the battle.

William Harbutt died of pneumonia in 1921, aged seventy-seven, on a business trip to New York. The Bathampton factory continued to flourish for another fifty years.

What he could not have foreseen was the many novel applications from developing industries for his invention. In the Second World War Blanchard was again called upon by the War Office, this time to reproduce Ordnance Survey maps in three-dimensional form. At the start of the Cold War, when the French, American and British zones of a divided Berlin were blockaded by the Soviet Union, the allies were forced to fly coal into the parts of the city they controlled. To prevent coal dust escaping from the aircraft holds Plasticine was used to seal the flooring.

As part of its research into atomic energy, the government, through its Ministry of Supply, commissioned Harbutt's to research the possibility of developing a new kind of Plasticine that would flow like cream when heated to 81°F. The world's first spacesuit was modelled in Plasticine.

Steel manufacturers used it to measure stress. Blanchard made a 'racing driver' for Sir Malcolm Campbell before his attempt on a land speed record. Placed in a wind tunnel with pressure equivalent to 200 miles per hour it showed how a real driver might be blown out of his seat. Explosive experts used it for demolition practice. Surgeons used it when rehearsing difficult operations. Tree surgeons used it when grafting or protecting cut surfaces.

Children, or their parents, were always the best customers. Instead of the educational sets such as the 'Add a Bit Modelling Game', priced half-a-crown that William had devised, there were now Mr Men, Muppets, Captain Scarlet or Tom and Jerry sets to test their dexterity.

In 1970 the Bathampton mill was destroyed in a fire caused by faulty equipment supplied to Harbutt's. A modern factory was constructed to replace the old, paid for after a protracted legal battle by the guilty party's insurers. It may not have been a sign from heaven, but the event happened at a moment when the ways children approached play were changing. First colour television, then Playstations and computers held more charms for them than the tacky material that often ended up full of grit and fluff rolled into a shapeless wad or stuck to the living-room carpet. The company was taken over.

The brand may have vanished, but the generic, Plasticine, continued to be made and sold. One of the less catchy slogans that Harbutt's had coined was 'Who kneads plasticine?'. The answer was a group of grown-ups who recognised its potential for cartoon figurines and then, a natural progression, 'claymation', that is, their extended use in animated movies.

One of the first graphic designers to try out the medium was the pop artist Alan Aldridge, best known for his work on Beatle record covers, who was commissioned to sculpt seven one-foot high Conservative party ministers for a Labour election campaign, the implication being that they were seven political dwarves.

Aardman Animations, started by Peter Lord and David Sproxton, began making short films in the middle of the 1970s. In an interview with the professional magazine *Animation World*, Lord was asked about the difference between the clay puppets that starred in his movies and the computer-generated images of cartoons: 'There is a fundamental difference', he replied 'between working with your hands and your arms and your fingertips, and working on the keyboard.

I don't know… For all of us animators at Aardman now, we are trained in this craft, just like a musician or a painter, it's all hand and head, hand and brain.'

It's a pure Swedenborgian answer that would have William Harbutt rolling over in his grave with delight.

Nick Park, creator of Aardman's *Wallace and Gromit*, can recall making worms out of clay in his garden before he could read or write. On his first day at infant school he made a train out of Plasticine. Unconsciously, adults warm to the care that has gone into every one of Wallace's movements, relating them to their own botched efforts when young. Children who may no longer play with it at home, have certainly done so in the classroom. They respond to the surreal, child-like imagination of the action because it matches their own.

There's a story that William Harbutt was riding downhill in a pony and trap. One of the wheels came loose and went spinning past him. 'What's that?' he asked the driver, completely unperturbed. It's an image that Nick Park would know how to animate to perfection.

23

HORSTMAN…N

Labourers demolishing parts of a garage near Kingsmead Square in 1970 were asked to pull down a disused air-raid shelter. Almost as soon as they pierced the concrete floor with a jack hammer they noticed they were boring into a void. Through the hole, the workmen caught glimpses of a secret underground depot of aircraft engines, wings, propellers, stretchers, first-aid kits, helmets, even an antiquated lorry. It took them three months and fifty skip-loads to clear the site.

The garage's previous owners had been the Horstman Motor Works, a firm whose history is, if anything, as strange as the forgotten cache.

Gustav Horstmann, a German clock maker, settled in Bath in the middle of the nineteenth century. Ambitious, creative, he invented the world's first precision micrometer, accurate to one thousandth of an inch (it's tucked away in the Science Museum). His next venture was to

The Horstmann family.

design and manufacture a self-winding clock whose mechanism was linked to barometric pressure. One of the two examples he made, functional rather than decorative, is displayed in the Bath at Work Museum.

Sidney Adolph, his younger son, must have taken after him because he was sent to work as an assistant to John Hippisley, an amateur inventor and member of the Royal Society with homes in Lansdown Crescent and at Ston Easton near Bristol, who had worked on a diamond cutter for engraving glass. While there, Sidney saw his first electric torch and more significantly, his first petrol engine.

Sidney Horstmann put the first time switches in Bath's street lights.

Moving along the old boy network, Sidney went next to London where he was employed by Colonel Rookes Evelyn Bell Crompton. This imposing ex-soldier, was among the pioneers of electric lighting technology. His company, Crompton & Co. produced virtually every electrical device of the day – instruments, domestic appliances and lamps – and was also the first major British manufacturer of generators. Its power station at Kensington Court, from 1887, provided the first practical house-to-house electrical-supply scheme.

Returning to Bath, where his father and brother, Otto, were still making timepieces, Sidney used components from the next-door cycle shop in Union Street to build himself a kind of electrically driven machine, steered like a Bath chair, with a tiller.

As an interesting aside, in later life he claimed that he had been given the first speeding ticket in England while driving near the Royal Crescent some time around the turn of the century.

The Red Flag Act of 1865, which insisted upon two drivers and a person walking sixty yards in front of any horseless carriage had set a speed limit of two miles per hour, but it had been repealed in 1896 and there was an overall maximum limit of fourteen miles per hour. According to Sidney, he had been testing a hydraulic braking system on the hill by Marlborough Buildings when the pipe split and the fluid spilled out.

The police constable who arrested Sidney takes up the story: 'I was standing at the junction when I noticed a vehicle approaching at the fantastic pace of approximately 19 mph. When I ordered it to stop, it took no notice.'

Apparently, the bobby didn't believe Sidney's explanation. Nor did the court that fined him.

His interest in the commercial applications of electricity and light may have been what brought him into contact with two other local innovators. John Rudge's 'biophantoscope' was a kind of magic lantern that could view a series of images in rapid succession. William Friese-Green had a fashionable photographic shop. The latter, inspired by his friend's instrument, made himself a strip of perforated celluloid film and fitted it inside a camera that had been doctored by adding a crank handle and, having set it up on a tripod at the top of Piccadilly, London, filmed the first moving pictures with Sidney standing as an onlooker.

The upshot of his technological breakthrough was that Friese-Green went bankrupt, sold his patent and spent the rest of his career on the fringes of an ever-expanding movie industry.

Perhaps learning from his friend's example, Sidney, ensured that his ideas, even those that may eventually have failed, reached the market. As the new century broke, with the help of his brother he sold an automatic timer for gas street lighting to the council. The city was waking up, constructing an electric tramway system. An old-fashioned coach builder, S.A. Fuller, in Kingsmead Square, was signing contracts with the new Rolls Royce company to build the bodywork for its cars.

Sidney may already have fancied himself as a motor manufacturer. For the time being he had to content himself with patenting and selling motorcycle gears through the company he had formed. By 1913, though, he was ready to launch his own Horstmann automobile. He converted an ex-dance hall into a factory housing the Horstmann Motor Co. This wasn't exactly a headline event. The year's new models, for example, included the Armstrong, Athmac, Autocrat, Autotrix and Averies – and that's just the ones beginning with the letter A. His three-speed, four-cylinder, 995cc lightweight car, kick-started by a foot pedal (as opposed to the conventional handle that had to be cranked) and with a tool kit fitted as standard, did have enough design attractions to sway the judges at the Crystal Palace Motor Show in 1913, who awarded it their prize for 'Car with the most novel features'.

It had barely gone into production before war broke out.

Sidney's immediate problem was protecting his street light time switches, by winning a libel suit against a competitor, the sententiously named British Foreign and Colonial Automatic Light Control Co. of Bournemouth, for posting circulars alleging that Horstmann was a German company and disloyal to the Crown. He won his case. The manufacture of armament tools at the car plant, particularly those related to the new tanks, would even earn Sidney an OBE, but the accusation left its mark because, the war over, he dropped the final 'n' of his surname and, although the gear and light-switch manufacturing side of the business retained it, the Horstman car copied the way Sidney now signed himself.

After the armistice, automobile production slowly started again, with the assembly of the pre-war model. This wasn't successful, so he

A Horstmann car – sporty, but not quite fast enough to win Le Mans.

decided to buy in engines, rather than redesign them and changed the chassis to fit them. His choice fell on a reliable workhorse that had earned its reputation by powering the explorer Ernest Shackleton's tractors across Antarctica, the Coventry Simplex – later developed into the Coventry Climax.

As an alternative, he offered a sporty car fitted with an Anzani engine. Alessandro Anzani, an Italian mechanic, had made his reputation through his collaboration with Louis Bleriot, the aircraft pioneer who was the first aviator to fly the Channel, but Horstman would have known him first as a motorcycle designer. His British subsidiary had branched out into motor-vehicle engines, particularly for the fast, light sports cars such as the Morgan and the Fraser Nash.

Most Horstmans were open-bodied two- or four-seaters, although a customised saloon model was listed in 1921. There was a very raffish Super Sports option too, armed with an external exhaust pipe, pointed tail and polished aluminium body. It was the high era of motor racing at the Brooklands track. Sidney's racing cars, entered, competed manfully, but never won. In France they took part in road races at Le Mans, but never managed to last the distance. Even racing his own cars didn't help Sidney. At the time his advertising carried the slogan: 'The car that passes you'. Unfortunately, on the racetrack, too many of the other competitors passed him.

Ever an innovator, he experimented with superchargers, was the first UK manufacturer to fit Lockheed hydraulic brakes to all four wheels and, in 1925, to use cellulose paintwork. Sales, however, were dwindling, despite the car appealing to women drivers because the wheels were easy to change. Although there were still less than 2 million motorised vehicles on the road, compared to the 28 million of the present day, he had probably built and sold under a thousand when he wound up the company. Production lines of T Model Fords and Austin 7s were squeezing out all but a privileged few car makers. Forced into liquidation, he re-floated it, attempted to introduce a saloon, christened the Pulteney, and as a last gesture custom-built an experimental Silver Car with all round coil sprung (as opposed to 'leaves') suspension and a saloon body finished in aluminium cellulose paint that was driven for 250,000 miles without ever being put into production.

In the automobile world nobody had bothered with spring suspension before he introduced it. Five years later the major manufacturers took up the idea. Even if it was by chance, as an engineer he was ahead of his time.

The 'coil-spring suspension' supplied the basis for an idea that would outlast his ill-fated automobile. George Carwardine was one of the engineers on whom Horstman had relied to bring this technologically advanced idea to fruition. Once the company had renounced its plans to develop any new models, he struck out on his own. While working for Sidney he had conceived of a way in which springs could be used to counterpoise each other so that two articulated 'arms' could hold an object in a stable position. He decided to exploit the system by applying it to a work light. To make it he needed a specialist spring manufacturer, so he approached a company, Terry, which agreed not just to supply the springs but to adopt his concept. It was meant to be called the Equipoise, but the patent office wasn't disposed to register the trademark. So it was called the Anglepoise instead.

While his glamorous sports cars were falling behind, Sidney was doing good business with suspension for the Light Mk I tanks that the military was specifying. The family's more mundane Horstmann Gear Co. was supplying street-light timers around the world: 'They sell because they excel.'

So long as Horstman…n stuck to what it or rather they knew best, it / they thrived. The compulsion to invent was never far away. A gas pistol, an anaesthetic vaporiser, pet clippers and, latterly, an unforgettable barber's shears that hoovered up the hair as it trimmed the short back and sides.

At the end of the Second World War (three Horstmanns died on the second night of the Bath Blitz (see chapter 24) the companies that Sidney had formed were swept up in the merger game of pass the parcel. His motor company passed from owner to owner. It briefly owned, in a strange twist of fate, Coventry Climax, who had once made the engines for its cars. Horstman Defence Systems, its current trading name, still in Bath, still makes components for tanks. Horstmann Gears has changed gear to become Horstmann Controls and Timers, Bristol based, making electronic timers rather than the tick-tocks that were once fitted to lampposts.

Sidney, of course, has joined the league of blue-sky inventors. Unlike Colonel Crompton, or John Hippisley he never made it to the Royal Society, or its obituary columns. He never won Le Mans, but his influence permeates many aspects of our lives, such as when we walk beneath a street lamp, or set the timer on the central-heating system. To use a cliché, he was very much a chip off the old block, like Papa Gustav, the inventor, who channelled all his energies into inventing a self-winding clock that we now take for granted.

And what happened to all those aircraft parts, helmets and stretchers unearthed by the labourers? Nobody knows… maybe they went underground again.

24

BAEDEKER BLITZ

It may sound a little churlish to blame Sir Winston Churchill for the bombing of Bath in 1942, but he has to shoulder some of the responsibility. Early that year he had listened to one of his advisers, Lord Cherwell, who had suggested that 'dehousing' was likely to lower German morale. This nasty euphemism for deliberately flattening civilian homes, struck a cord with the prime minister, who announced a policy to 'make the enemy burn and bleed in every way'.

Newly appointed head of Bomber Command, Vice Air Marshall Arthur Harris, had the task, one he undertook willingly, of implementing his leader's wishes. He is remembered for the 1,000-bomber raid on Cologne and the firestorm that killed up to 100,000 Dresden inhabitants. His earliest attempt at area bombing that deliberately targeted non-combatants was an attack on the Baltic seaport of Lubeck.

It was chosen for sound tactical reasons. Poorly defended, near the coast, it would be easy to hit with minimal aircraft losses. It was a medieval town with houses clustered together: fire would spread rapidly, would be hard to control. On 28 March 1942, 234 RAF planes, to use the jargon of the day, 'browned' it, destroying most of the centre.

It was clear from the attack, which had made little attempt to hit the port, that the British had meant to destroy Lubeck and had done so. Hitler was incandescent with rage, sending a directive to the Luftwaffe High Command to carry out terror attacks of a retaliatory nature on towns other than London. The immediate riposte was a series of 'tip-and-run' attacks on seaside resorts – Torquay, Exmouth, Swanage, Bognor Regis – by fast fighter bombers.

Then, on 23 April, a flight of twenty-five bombers hit Exeter. The raid was a coup for the Nazi propaganda machine, whose spokesman, Gustav Braun Von Stumm, announced: 'We shall go out and bomb every building in Britain marked with three stars in the Baedeker Guide.' In its day, the guide had the authority of, say, a modern Michelin or Lonely Planet, except that it rarely awarded more than two stars to any site of cultural interest. Bath, though, was one of these.

The spa had been relatively unscathed until then; the odd stray bomb to fall had probably been intended for neighbouring Bristol. Except for the Admiralty's offices and the engineering firm Stothert & Pitt that made tank parts it was in strategic terms a backwater. Nor did it have any defences. It had no ack-ack batteries, no barrage balloons. Searchlights on the top of Lansdown Hill and Claverton Down had been placed there for the protection of Bristol.

Its location, surrounded by an amphitheatre of hills, made it impossible to miss, especially given the rules of engagement that drew no distinction between the smart residences of the Circus or the crescents and the working-class quarters strung out on either side of the River Avon.

The kind of force at the Luftwaffe's disposal bore no relation to the massive power that it had mustered for the London Blitz. Germany was fighting Russia on its Eastern Front and had transferred the bulk of its bomber fleet there. Flights of Dornier 217s and Junker 88s, fighter-bombers stationed in Northern France and the Low Countries spent much of their flying time harassing shipping. They had been used effectively to bomb Exeter, and on 25 April they would provide the spearhead of the assault on Bath. Supported by some old aircraft belonging to a training squadron and a few older Heinkel 111s that carried updated electronic equipment designed to follow a radio beam to a given target, they made up a force of about eighty aircraft.

The planned assault involved two phases. The Heinkels would fly in ahead, using parachute flares and incendiaries to light up the target. They would be followed in by the main bomber formations which would drop their payloads, return to their French airfields, refuel and return to bomb the burning city a second time.

A German reporter aboard one of the bombers recorded the wounding of the city from the air. He called it an 'annihilation'. It wasn't that so much as a brutal introduction to total war:

We roar down from the sky, now the first flares from our leaders light up the land like day! Beneath, the River Avon winds through the country like a silver thread. Here below us is the great loop in the middle of which lies the town, and now too the first small incendiaries go dow. Suddenly, in front of us a great towering flame appears which dazzles us with its flaming red, even in the cockpit! A huge cloud bursts up from below, sinisterly illuminated by the greedy, self-devouring flames... We go down still lower, and beneath us we see rows of burning houses. Smoke rises from them and thickens into a black cloud which lies over the town like a pall. We can recognise the streets as well, fire and destruction are raging in them!

At ground level, the picture was very different: stricken streets closed, churches in ruins, civil defence hose-pipes mingling with tangled telephone wires fallen across the roads, torn-up tramlines, vans and lorries collecting people to drive them to the safety of surrounding villages, rumours flying about as to what had been hit and who killed.

During the fifty-minute raid, the planes flew so low that witnesses on the ground could see the pilots. They strafed the streets at random, hoping to keep the civil defence and fire brigade from responding to the blazes that had sprang up. However, there was no firestorm: Bath, unlike Lubeck, wasn't built of wood. A direct hit by a 250-kilogram high-explosive bomb demolished Roseberry Road where it landed on an Anderson shelter. Thirty people died in the street. Incendiaries gutted the Assembly Rooms.

Their mission a success, the *Luftflotte* returned to its landing fields in Normandy and Britanny, refuelled, rearmed and returned to Bath, pasting it, if anything, more ferociously than before.

The cost had been negligible: five or six planes shot down or crashing and a few severely damaged. It hadn't been a good night for the RAF. Fifty-one 'Cat's Eye' Hurricanes that had been sent to patrol grids of 'searchlight boxes' never so much as contacted the raiders. Three squadrons of Beaufort night fighters had little more luck. They had been thwarted by the Luftwaffe pilots, jinking, diving, circling and flying low over the city, making it impossible for them to lock their radar on to the fast Dornier 217s and Junker 88s. An eyewitness on Odd Down saw the enemy planes flying below his eyeline, almost touching the rooftops.

To compound the RAF's problems, their on-board electronics caused interference with ground-control tracking systems. Perhaps more significant still, one squadron had converted from Defiants to Beauforts four days earlier and its pilots had barely familiarised themselves with the controls. The next morning the Nazi High Command didn't have to distort the facts when it issued an upbeat communiqué, taken from an eyewitness account, boasting of a victory:

> Thousands of explosive and incendiary bombs, often from a low altitude, were dropped on Bath all of which exploded in the target area. Countless incendiaries were dropped and then blazing fires broke out, especially in the centre. The attack, which was carried out in waves, went entirely according to plan, and repaid the British for their wanton destruction of living quarters, cultural monuments and welfare arrangements in ancient German cities.

If the RAF Fighter Command's defences had proved ineffectual, its area bombing policy had continued with the targeting of a second Baltic town, Rostock. There, it had flown four successive sorties between 23 and 26 April. Almost missing its objective, the Old City, at its first attempt, it had improved its aim with each attempt so that, by the end of the fourth night, it had destroyed 130 acres, about two-thirds of the town. Over 500 assorted bombers, Wellingtons, Stirlings, Whitleys and Lancasters had taken part with 8 planes shot down.

In this tit-for-tat battle of attrition, Bath had to expect a further beating. It came fourteen hours after the previous night's bombardment at the same time as the British force was winging its way to the Baltic to finish the job on Rostock.

The scenario of Bath's second blitz echoed the night before. It was clear and moonlit over the city. The enemy crossed the Channel after midnight, formed up over South Devon and, avoiding the Bristol anti-aircraft batteries, flew to their target, again meeting almost no opposition. The operational failure of the Hurricanes the night before persuaded the RAF to leave them on the ground this time. Based at Colerne, 125 Squadron switched back to Defiants, the planes they had been flying before the delivery of their new Beauforts, but with no better result. One gunner who managed to line his sights on an enemy plane couldn't pull the trigger because his gun's 'fire safe' mechanism was missing. Another pilot's intercom wasn't working and he wasn't able to join the fray. A third Defiant's undercarriage snapped off on landing.

Two days later ack-ack batteries were set up on Lansdown and at South Stoke, but by then the Luftwaffe had moved on to other Baedeker sites – Norwich, York and Canterbury.

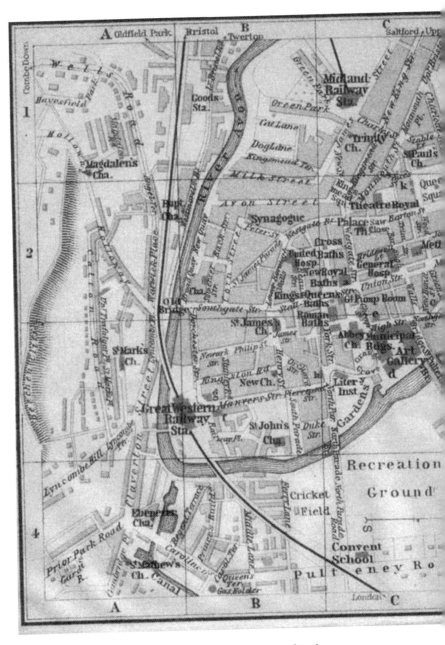

Pre-Second World War Baedeker map of Bath.

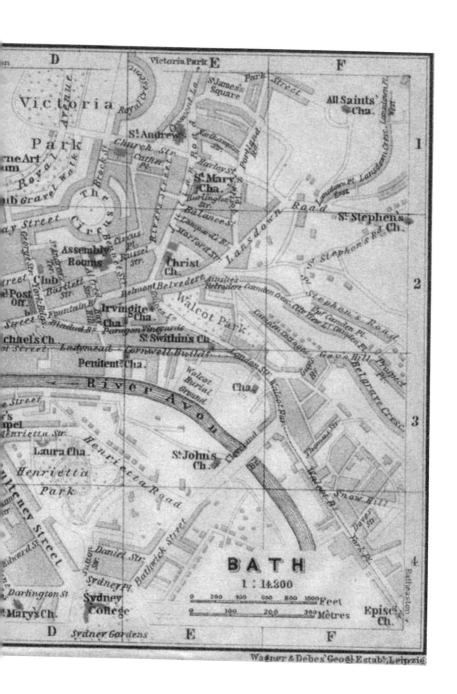

BATH

1 : 14,300

0   200   400   600   800   1000 Feet

0   100   200   300 Mètres

Joseph Goebbels, Hitler's propaganda chief, reported in his diary that the Führer was delighted with the way in which his air force was carrying the war to the British:

> He said he would repeat these raids night after night until the English were sick and tired of terror attacks. He shares my opinion absolutely that cultural centres, health resorts and civilian resorts must be attacked now. There is no other way of bringing the English to their senses. They belong to a class of human beings with whom you can only talk after you have first knocked out their teeth.

Over 400 had died in the three waves of attack, more than any other city to suffer during the Baedeker Blitz. For the inhabitants it had been terrifying, especially those living in the poorer housing on the western fringes, which was the most heavily damaged. Some 30 fires had broken out on day one, 90 on day two when 8,000 incendiaries had fallen. A 16-year-old member of the rescue squad recalled tunnelling through the debris of what had once been the Regina Hotel opposite the Assembly Rooms: 'Because I was the smallest and thinnest, I had to try to find out if anybody was still alive in there.

Bomb damage in Queen's Square.

I managed to get to the end of the tunnel and found 26 people there, all dead.' Among the Bath fatalities were a retired brigadier, a schoolmaster, a masseur, a cabinet-maker and a gravedigger. In a blanket attack on a civilian population, survival is a matter of luck. In the Roseberry Road blast, a three-year-old child blown out of the shelter had been unscathed, while those about her had been killed or maimed.

Some 900 buildings had been written off, almost 12,500 damaged, but the total could have been far worse, especially for the city's historic architecture. The Abbey suffered only minor damage. Three bombs landed close to the Circus, damaging properties, but none beyond repair. Camden Crescent, too, was hit, but not so badly that any buildings had to be demolished. The Royal Crescent survived intact, Lansdown Crescent too. The Francis Hotel in Queen Square received a direct hit, was demolished and rebuilt after the war.

The argument for area bombing on both sides had been that it would destroy morale. In the case of Bath it didn't work. When no more bombs fell the next day, people who had moved out began to return. A poem written a month after the blitz caught the residue of anger that was felt, but also the attack's pointlessness:

They came, they loosed their loads, leaving behind
Insensate havoc and slaughter, futile crime.

25

JUDGING A BOOK BY ITS COVER

Arrive by train and the first experience you'll have of Bath is of Manvers Street, pointing like an arrow towards the centre close by the Abbey. With a police station on the right; a bus station, functional office blocks, snack bars and budget hotels on the left; the view isn't pretty. It's not somewhere to linger, so why do so many casual passers-by stop outside the sober façade of Bayntun's?

It's a bookshop, so much is obvious. It's also a lot more than that. Gilt, leather-bound first editions in the window have the tactile charm of fresh éclairs in an old-fashioned baker's window.

The front door is locked. A sign, almost a challenge, invites you to ring the bell. Do so. Step inside, into a room of mahogany desks and cabinets packed with neat rows of books. It could be austere, like going into a Dickensian headmaster's study, but isn't; it's soothing – like stroking a well-bred Labrador.

Four generations of Bayntuns have bound books. Opening his business in 1894, George, the founder, quickly realised that he could make more profit buying books, restoring them and reselling them than by covering magazines or other cheaply produced works for private customers, how other local binders scraped a living. Craft binderies were closing down.

Just before the start of the Second World War, he acquired Riviere, a venerable company that was already established when Victoria came to the throne. With it came a collection of over 10,000 antique 'tools', used to impress designs on leather.

The aftermath of war left Bayntun's languishing in a slow decline. It might have succumbed (most craft binders already had), except for the energy of George's daughter Constance, who had succeeded him after his death during the war. She made way for her son who, in turn, has been followed by Edward.

George had moved from his workshop in Walcot Street after purchasing Riviere into the present premises that had been the postal sorting office. Behind the respectable front room was the factory floor

Bayntun's handbound copy of Kipling's *Just So Stories*.

where the arcane process of dismantling, stitching, covering, pressing, binding and decorating took – takes – place.

The pages you have in front of you as you read this have been formed at the press of a computer button, cut, collated and manu-factured, admittedly to a high standard so they don't fall apart if you happen to be reading them on a beach or in a train, by machine. It takes ten hours' work, spread over days, for a team of craftsmen to bind a single Bayntun's book.

For those who work there, it's a job for life. The two sisters in the

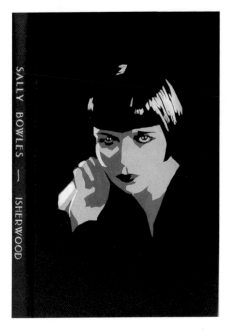

stitching room joined in 1968 and their daughters are learning the ropes. Of the binders, one started in 1947 and the other in 1945. The youngest person to work there isn't far short of thirty.

What kinds of books pass through their hands? Ones with no commercial value at all except to the clients who bring them in, priceless antiquarian objects in need of restoration, tatty first editions whose value will increase with a leather-bound cover, special work for collectors, a few hundred tomes each year of which maybe 100 will be kept as stock.

Binders were more closely linked to booksellers than printers, when James Riviere opened his Bath shop in 1829. The title page on an edition would say 'Printed by ——' followed by the name of the seller. The latter commissioned binders to cover the bulk of the copies he received in a variety of styles so that a purchaser could buy a bound copy off the peg. Alternatively he could commission a bespoke one of his own.

According to Edward Bayntun-Coward, his father borrowed elements of this traditional link and revived the firm's fortunes by buying up first editions in need of repair and turning them into desirable objects: 'He would drive to Salisbury for the day, returning with a car full of books.' These were the raw materials that pulled apart, recovered, polished and gilded formed his stock in trade.

Authors like Jane Austen, out of fashion a generation ago, and so easily collected and readily replaceable, are once again popular. Now, a set of her works bound in the Bayntun workshop fetches £10,000. Edward says he keeps a couple in stock in case you are interested. He could also supply Ian Fleming's James Bond series for the same amount.

Price and value, though, are fluctuating elements in an insoluble equation. Edward recalled how he attended an auction where one first edition *Alice in Wonderland* in poor repair fetched £200; a copy 'Bound by Bayntun-Riviere' made exactly ten times as much. And yet, the same book in perfect order would be worth many times this to an obsessive collector. He knows. He spent four years as personal buyer for the billionaire Paul Getty jnr who never bought a book as an investment. 'If someone came in with *The Great Gatsby* in mint condition with a dust jacket, I'd tell him it's a £150,000 book and shouldn't be touched. A shabby one might be worth £1000. At auction in one of our new bindings, collectors would probably bid £5000.'

In his father's or great-grandfather's era, Harrod's or Asprey's, the luxury retailers, were major customers. That's changed. Whether through a direct approach or via the Internet, nearly all contacts are with individuals. One recently bought all seventy-two Agatha Christie crime novels, the pulp fiction of their day. An American couple who own three houses ordered *Works of Thomas Hardy* for their three libraries in blue, red and green bindings.

Restoring or rebinding a book that a private person brings in is usually charged by the inch. Edward says that a duchess who has brought him her books for decades complains volubly about the prices. His response is that if she takes her car to be serviced, a mechanic, maybe fresh out of college will do the job in a morning, whereas what she receives from him will last centuries: 'You could chuck one of our books out of a first floor window. Its structure and cover would remain as one. I've come across pre-1900 bindings of ours and I'm sure they would survive for all time.'

The technique of making a book hasn't really changed since Beau Nash's day. What's unique to Bayntun's is that it still applies the same

Pressing before fitting the binding.

methods and materials as then, down to a gelatine-like glue prepared from ground animal bones: 'We are the only binder in the world which still edge-gilds by hand.'

Whether they are 'quarter', 'half' or 'full' leather, Bayntun's books are about the look and touch of goatskin: 'Morocco'. It's called this because it used to come almost exclusively from North Africa. Now it may have started life on a Nigerian billy or an Indonesian nanny, and the finest, with its vegetable-dyed natural grain, is increasingly difficult to come by. Ironically, this is the result of letting the flocks roam more widely than was once the case. Edward frequently rejects skins that have been delivered to him. Pelts may be gnarled like an old organic potato or scratched.

A good book is more than paper held together with leather-coated cardboard, expensively bound and embossed. It has to open well, sit well in the hand. Everyone who reads cut-price paperbacks is familiar with words merging into the gutter, illegible until the book is pulled apart.

Founder George's motto had been: 'A good book in a good binding'. It's the leitmotiv of a process that seems very strange by the standards of our automated world.

The painstaking labour involved in rebuilding some diseased copies has one reaching for words like 'Lazarus', 'raising' and 'dead'. By com-

A flat iron makes a convenient weight.

parison, most modern makeovers are laughable impostures.

It begins in what is facetiously known as the 'Girls' Room'. A large table takes up most of the space. On it lie pages in a state of undress; string, needles, paste, sandpapers and erasers. Work is about to start on a first edition of, say, *Goldfinger*, that has been in store waiting to be rebound. The back and the boards are taken off, the first of 100 steps before the book will be ready for sale.

The pages must be cleaned, by washing or sanding them, before they can be formed and hand-stitched with linen cord to give strength. Marble end papers are also pasted to cartridge paper that will be stuck to the boards when the book is fitted together again. Binding has its own mysterious vocabulary of which 'forwarding' is a catch-all to describe what happens after the book passes out of the Girls' Room.

Its spine is brushed with glue and left to set before the two edges are hammered until they form a neat bevel. The pages now go into a press that creates grooves, the thickness of the boards on the shoulders, either side of the bevels. Are we following closely?

Next the boards are fitted into place, with cords slipped through them and the book is weighted overnight to fix its shape. After the edges of the board have been trimmed and the spine tapped into shape, the edges of the paper are ready for gilding.

Working with gold leaf is notoriously unpredictable. If the weather is too hot, too cold, too damp, too dry, it may not stick. Even after a lifetime's experience, the binder can have accidents. To prevent pages sticking together, they're dusted with French chalk similar to that used by a gymnast before performing on parallel bars. The edges are rubbed with a red clay that helps the gold to adhere. Then each leaf is picked up with a badger-hair brush known as a gilder's tip. Egg white mixed with water helps to stick the gold leaf in place. When it has dried it's burnished initially with a bloodstone, finally with a squirrel-hair brush.

To complete the spine's preparation, silk headbands are sewn along its top and bottom as an additional strengthening. A strip of muslin is pasted to it and a hollow tube of paper that acts as a buffer is laid on top. Decorative bands are placed over the spine and the book is set aside for covering with leather.

A skin of natural grain, Morocco, is cut to size and painted with paste before being fastened and pressed into position over the boards and spine in a single piece. Extra paper is stuck to the insides of the boards, they're turned back to back and left to dry for a day, before the book is ready to be weighted in a press for another two weeks, like a

Gold leaf being tooled.

Some of the 10,000 nineteenth-century tools that Bayntun still uses.

cheddar cheese, after which the leather is polished with a hot iron, cleaned with vinegar and dried again. More strips of gold leaf are placed round the turn-ins before the end papers that were cut to shape weeks before, can be stuck down and left to dry.

How much craftsmanship goes into the decoration of a book depends on the customer's wishes. At the simplest level, the lettering of a title will be impressed onto the spine with a heated type holder and brushed with glair before applying the gold. Elaborate design may be stamped onto the boards, the spine or the turn-ins with tools that are unique to the bindery, some dating back to the early days of James Riviere. Whatever the chosen pattern, each touch of gold needs wiping with a warm rag moistened with olive oil and the leather will receive a light French polish before it leaves the shop.

The care lavished on the presentation on this volume of *Goldfinger* will have turned it into an object worthy of the eponymous anti-hero himself. Ian Fleming's James Bond story is the same whatever the edition, whatever the copy's state. What Bayntun's craftsmen have done is turn the printed word into a treasure, one that is quite possibly worth its weight in gold.